ON BEING AND ESSENCE

ST. THOMAS AQUINAS

ON BEING AND ESSENCE

Translated with an Introduction and Notes

by

ARMAND MAURER, C.S.B.

SECOND REVISED EDITION

THE PONTIFICAL INSTITUTE OF MEDIAEVAL STUDIES

TORONTO, CANADA

1968

CONTENTS

PRINTED BY UNIVERSA - WETTEREN - BELGIUM

INTRODUCTION

Throughout the long history of Western philosophy —
from Parmenides to Heidegger — metaphysicians have
tried to fathom the meaning of being. What does it mean
to be or to exist? This is both the easiest and most difficult
question to answer. Who can fail to know the existence or
non-existence of the things he experiences? At the same time
who would claim to have plumbed the depths of the meaning
of existence? Especially at moments of crisis in human life,
such as birth and death, the mystery of existence forcefully
imposes itself upon us. We recognize then that it is not a
problem admitting of an exhaustive and definitive solution
(as we may solve a mathematical puzzle) but a mystery
we can never fully comprehend.[1]

It is perhaps understandable under these circumstances
that some modern philosophers have given up the inquiry
into being, proclaiming with Nietzsche that the word is
nothing but "a vapor and a fallacy."[2] Whereas for Thomas
Aquinas, following a long Judeo-Christian tradition, being
is the name of God, Nietzsche, the passionate opponent of
this tradition, saw in being "the last cloudy streak of eva-
porating reality."[3] In the wake of Nietzsche's criticism,
the central question for philosophy today, as Heidegger

---

[1] For the distinction between problem and mystery, see Jacques Maritain,
A Preface to Metaphysics (London, 1943), pp. 3-9; Gabriel Marcel, *The
Philosophy of Existence* (New York, 1949), pp. 1-31, *The Mystery of Being*,
2 vols. (Chicago, 1950).
[2] Friedrich Nietzsche, *The Twilight of the Idols* (*Nietzsche's Complete Works*,
New York and London, 1911, 16, pp. 19, 22). Following Martin Heidegger,
An Introduction to Metaphysics, trans. R. Manheim (New York, 1959), p. 29.
Sidney Hook argues that "we can banish the term 'being' from the vocabulary
of philosophy." *The Quest for Being* (New York, 1961), p. 147.
[3] Quoted by M. Heidegger, *ibid*.

observes, is: "Is being a mere word and its meaning a vapor, or does what is designated by the word 'being' hold within it the spiritual destiny of the West?"[4]

If it is true, as Heidegger goes on to say, that "we have fallen away from what this word says and for the moment cannot find our way back,"[5] with disastrous consequences for our civilization, can we do better than turn to the great masters of metaphysics in the Western tradition and put to them Heidegger's question: "How does it stand with being?"

The short treatise of St. Thomas *On Being and Essence* is a classic in this metaphysical tradition. It was one of his first works, written before March 1256, when he became Master of Theology at Paris.[6] He was then slightly more than thirty years old. Fr. Roland-Gosselin, one of the editors of the Latin text, offers evidence that St. Thomas wrote it while composing the first book of his *Scripta* on the *Sentences* of Peter Lombard, which he began about 1252.[7] Indeed, there is a close affinity between this work and *On Being and Essence* both in their metaphysical notions and in their dependence on Avicenna, the Arabian philosopher who at

---

[4] M. Heidegger, *op. cit.*, p. 35. I have translated Heidegger's German term 'geistige' as 'spiritual' and not 'historical', as in Manheim's translation. See p. 31.

[5] *Op. cit.*, p. 33. Heidegger asks, "What if it were possible that man, that nations in their greatest movements and traditions, are linked to being and yet had long fallen out of being, without knowing it, and that this was the most powerful and most central cause of their decline?" *Op. cit.*, p. 30.

[6] See M. D. Chenu, *Toward Understanding St. Thomas*, trans. A. M. Landry and D. Hughes (Chicago, 1964), p. 330; Vernon Bourke, *Aquinas' Search for Wisdom* (Milwaukee, 1965), p. 73.

[7] M. D. Roland-Gosselin, "Introduction" to *Le 'De Ente et Essentia' de S. Thomas d'Aquin* (Paris, 1926), pp. xxvi-xxviii. Following P. Mandonnet, Roland-Gosselin places the *Sentences* between 1254-1256, but St. Thomas may have begun lecturing on the *Sentences* in 1252. See W. A. Wallace, J. Weisheipl, "St. Thomas Aquinas," *The New Catholic Encyclopedia* (New York, 1967), 14, p. 104a.

that time was in vogue at Paris.[8] The *Scripta* on the *Sentences* is a helpful companion to *On Being and Essence*. It can be consulted with profit whenever there is difficulty in understanding the doctrine of the metaphysical treatise.

A product of St. Thomas' early career, *On Being and Essence* does not contain his mature metaphysical views. For his fully developed philosophy we must read his later writings, especially the *Disputed Questions*, *Summa Contra Gentiles*, and *Summa Theologiae*. These, however, are theological works in which metaphysics appears in a theological setting. Apart from his commentary on Aristotle's *Metaphysics*, whose main purpose is to expound the doctrine of Aristotle and not his personal views, *On Being and Essence* is his only purely metaphysical production. So it is of unique value in showing us how, as a young man, he understood and organized the fundamental notions of metaphysics.

There is little in this treatise that does not find a place in his mature works. The basic metaphysical themes he adopted at the beginning of his career remained the same throughout his life; yet he developed and deepened them as the years went by. Already in *On Being and Essence* he describes being (*esse*) as the actuality of essence,[9] the two forming a composition that results in a being (*ens*).[10] God has no other essence or nature than being; he is being in all its purity

---

[8] Avicenna is the Latin name of Ibn Sina (980-1037), a philosopher of Persian birth who taught at Bagdad. Some of his works (which he wrote in Arabic) were translated into Latin toward the end of the twelfth century and beginning of the thirteenth. For his doctrine of being, see M. D. Roland-Gosselin, *ibid.*, pp. 150-156; M. A. Goichon, *La Distinction de l'Essence et de l'Existence d'après Ibn Sina (Avicenne)* (Paris, 1937). For his influence on Western philosophy, see M. A. Goichon, *La Philosophie d'Avicenne et son Influence en Europe médiévale* (Paris, 1944).

[9] Chapter 4, § 8, p. 57.

[10] Chapter 4, § 2 and § 6, pp. 52, 56.

(*esse tantum*).[11] Creatures receive being as a participation of the divine being, their essences limiting the degree of this participation.[12] But nowhere in the treatise are we told that there is a *real* composition in creatures between their being and their essence, or that these two are *really* distinct. We must look to the other writings of St. Thomas for these clarifications. Neither does he make it explicit in this treatise that being (*esse*) is a more perfect actuality than form or essence, though this is implied in his statements. Only in his later works does he reach the height of his metaphysical powers and fully achieve the reformation in metaphysics that is associated with his name.[13]

At the center of this reformation is a new interpretation of being according to which (to quote St. Thomas) "to be (*esse*) is the actuality of all acts and consequently the perfection of all perfections."[14] In short, existence holds the primary place in the order of being. While not neglecting other aspects of being, such as form and essence, St. Thomas offers a radically new interpretation of being by emphasizing its existential side. This was a decisive moment in the history of Western metaphysics, for St. Thomas was transforming previous Greek and mediaeval conceptions of being, which gave primary place to form. Before St. Thomas, important progress had been made in the direction of an existential interpretation of being by the Arabian philosophers Alfarabi

---

[11] Chapter 4, § 6; chapter 5, § 2; pp. 55-56, 60-61.
[12] Chapter 5, § 4, p. 62.
[13] See Jacques Maritain, *A Preface to Metaphysics* (London, 1939), *Existence and the Existent* (New York, 1948); Etienne Gilson, *Being and Some Philosophers* (Toronto, 1952), *The Christian Philosophy of St. Thomas Aquinas* (New York, 1956), *Elements of Christian Philosophy* (New York, 1960); Gerald B. Phelan, "The Existentialism of St. Thomas," "The Being of Creatures," *G. B. Phelan: Selected Papers* (Toronto, 1967).
[14] St. Thomas, *De Potentia*, VII, 2, ad 9.

and Avicenna, and by the Christian theologian-philosopher William of Auvergne. But St. Thomas was the first to appreciate fully the supremacy of the act of existing over essence. *On Being and Essence* marks the beginning of this metaphysical reformation. Though heavily indebted to Aristotle, especially as interpreted by Avicenna, it reveals St. Thomas already beginning to go beyond them and to formulate his own metaphysical positions. It is not, however, his final word on the subject. Indeed, we can be sure that the treatise would have been quite different had he written it at the end of his career rather than at the beginning.

The occasion of the composition of the treatise is suggested by its dedication, recorded in several early catalogues of St. Thomas' works. Ptolemy of Lucca says that he wrote it "for his brethren and companions," and the compiler of another catalogue calls the treatise *On Being and Essence, for his Friar Associates.* These were probably his confrères at Saint James, the Dominican House of Studies in Paris, who were following his teaching and asked him to explain the fundamental notions of metaphysics.[15]

In the Prologue St. Thomas states the aim and scope of his work. He intends to explain the meaning of the terms 'a being' and 'an essence', how being and essence are found in the different orders of reality, and what relation they have to our logical notions of genus, species, and difference.

This states clearly enough that the purpose of the work is expository or explanatory. Answering the request of his young Dominican confrères, St. Thomas elucidates the meaning of certain key metaphysical notions, such as 'being', 'quiddity', 'form', 'nature', and 'essence'. But in clarifying

---

[15] M. D. Chenu, *op. cit.*, p. 330.

the language of metaphysics he is not concerned with words alone; he is defining names (*nomina*), and these are words with meaning. In short, they are signs, and as such they give us knowledge of the reality they signify. "A sound is a name," he says, "only insofar as it causes knowledge of reality, for a name is, as it were, a designation [of something]: *nomen non competit voci, nisi secundum quod facit notitiam de re, nomen enim dicitur quasi notamen.*"[16] Consequently the elucidation of the meaning of names (at least if they are names of reality) marks a progress in knowledge of the real world.

All names, whether written or spoken, signify things by means of concepts, and so they differ in signification as concepts do. Some concepts, called concepts of first intention, directly signify reality. Examples are 'man' and 'animal'. Other concepts, called concepts of second intention, are unlike them in that they do not directly signify reality or have an immediate foundation in it, but they are based on some activity of the mind in the course of knowing reality. Examples given by St. Thomas are logical and mathematical notions. The name 'genus', for instance, is not the sign of anything in reality, but it was devised as the name of a concept because it is predicable of many species. Finding that the concept 'animal' can be predicated of the species 'man' and 'dog', it is given the name 'genus'. Thus logical notions, like genus, species, and difference, do not have an immediate, but only a remote, foundation in reality. They are not concepts of reality but concepts of concepts, based on the mind's activity of relating concepts to each other in propositions.[17]

---

[16] *In IV Sent.*, d. 3, a. 2, 1, ad 9; ed. Moos, IV, p. 121. For the meaning of a name, see *In I Periher.*, lect. 4; ed. Leonine, I, pp. 19-22.

[17] For the distinction between first and second intentions, see below, p. 28, n. 3.

Unlike logical notions, those of metaphysics are first intentions: they signify reality and have their immediate foundation in it. Consequently the analysis of their meaning directly concerns reality itself.

The metaphysician's interest in the meaning of language is different from that of the etymologist. "The etymology of a word," St. Thomas writes, "differs from its meaning. For its etymology depends on what it is taken from for the purpose of signification, whereas its meaning depends on the thing to which it is applied for the purpose of signifying it. Now these differ sometimes: for *lapis* (a stone) takes its name from hurting the foot (*laedere pedem*), but this is not its meaning; otherwise iron, since it hurts the foot, would be a stone."[18]

Since the meaning of a word which is a sign of reality engages us with reality itself, it cannot be understood without grasping reality. Indeed, St. Thomas goes so far as to say that, although meaning (*ratio*) properly attaches to the concept of the mind (and hence is a term of second intention), nevertheless it may be said to be in reality "inasmuch as there is something in the real world corresponding to the mind's conception, as what is signified corresponds to a sign."[19] Hence the analysis and elucidation of metaphysical language must be distinguished from other types of linguistic studies; they are part of metaphysics as a science that aims to understand important features of the real world.

In chapter one St. Thomas begins by elucidating the metaphysical language of being. The most important terms here are *ens*, *esse*, and *essentia*: Latin words all derived from

---

[18] *Summa Theologiae*, II-II, 92, 1, ad 2. See I, 31, 1, ad 1.
[19] *In I Sent.*, d. 1, q. 1, a. 3; ed. Mandonnet, I, p. 67.

sum, which means 'I am'.[20] These are the most difficult terms in the treatise to understand and to translate into English. *Esse* is the infinitive of the verb *sum*, and it means simply 'to be'. *Ens* is the participial form, corresponding to the English 'being'. St. Thomas uses both as verbal nouns, and he explains their relationship as follows.[21] *Ens* is a concrete term, like *currens*. *Currens* signifies concretely 'one who is running' or 'a runner'; *ens* signifies concretely 'that which is'. As *currens* signifies a person along with his act of running, so *ens* signifies a subject as possessing an act of being or existing. This act of being, exercized by the subject, is expressed by the infinitive *esse*, as *currere* expresses the act of running. Both are abstract terms for they abstract from their subject. They are like the noun 'whiteness', which denotes the quality in abstraction from the subject of the quality. *Ens* resembles the concrete noun *album*, which means 'a white thing', expressing the subject as qualified by the color white. *Esse*, on the other hand, denotes only the act of being, in abstraction from the subject of the act.

This Latin metaphysical language has no adequate English equivalent. But perhaps we shall not betray the thought of St. Thomas, while observing the rules of good English, if we render *ens* as 'a being' and *esse* as 'being'.[22]

[20] For the history of the language of being, see E. Gilson, "Notes sur le Vocabulaire de l'Etre," *Mediaeval Studies*, 8 (1946), pp. 150-158.

[21] *In Boeth. de Hebd.*, c. 2; ed. Mandonnet, *Opuscula*, I, p. 171. See J. Owens, *St. Thomas and the Future of Metaphysics* (Milwaukee, 1957), p. 76, note 27; "The Accidental and Essential Character of Being in the Doctrine of St. Thomas Aquinas," *Mediaeval Studies*, 20 (1958), pp. 8-9.

[22] In translating *esse* as 'being' and *ens* as 'a being' I am following A. C. Pegis, *St. Thomas Aquinas: On the Truth of the Catholic Faith (Summa Contra Gentiles)*, Book One (New York, 1955), p. 50. On this point, see E. Gilson, *The Christian Philosophy of St. Thomas Aquinas*, p. 29; J. Owens, *ibid*. In another context, William Barrett points out the deficiency of English to translate the Latin couple *ens*, *esse*. He suggests that we use 'beings' to mean

When they are translated in this way, the reader is made aware that *esse* is the name of an act (the act of existing), as *currere* is the name of the act of running. At the same time the close relationship between *esse* and *ens* is maintained: *ens* ('a being') is in fact nothing but the concrete conceptualization of *esse* ('the act of being'). The word *ens* is derived from *esse* or *actus essendi*.[23] It is being (*esse*) that gives to a being (*ens*) its character of being, as it is running (*currere*) that gives to a runner (*currens*) his character of running. 'Existence' has not been used to translate *esse* because St. Thomas himself generally avoided its Latin counterpart *existentia*, no doubt because he thought the verbal noun *esse* better expressed the active character of being.

Another term related to *esse* is *essentia*. In St. Thomas' day it was customary to distinguish between two meanings of the term *esse*, the first existence or being, and the second essence or quiddity. William of Auvergne, for example, uses the term *esse* to denote both the existence of man and his intelligible and definable quiddity or essence.[24] Although the use of *esse* to mean essence had a long tradition in the Middle Ages, going back at least to Boethius,[25] St. Thomas

things that exist, and 'being' to mean the to-be of whatever is. See his *Irrational Man* (New York: Anchor Books, 1962), p. 212.

[23] *De Veritate*, I, 1; *Contra Gentiles*, I, 25, § 5.

[24] William of Auvergne, *De Trinitate*, 2 (Paris, 1674), supplementum, p. 2b. For his notion of being, see E. Gilson, "La notion d'existence chez Guillaume d'Auvergne," *Archives d'histoire doctrinale et littéraire du Moyen Age*, 15 (1946), pp. 55-91.

[25] Boethius identifies being (*esse*) with the form expressed by the definition. See his *In Isag. Por.*, IV, 14, editio secunda; CSEL 48, p. 273, lines 13-15. "The use of the infinitive of the verb 'to be' to denote a form or formal aspect of a thing goes back, in point of fact, to Aristotle," J. Owens, "The Accidental and Essential Character of Being in the Doctrine of St. Thomas Aquinas," *Mediaeval Studies*, 20 (1958), p. 14. St. Thomas occasionally reports the traditional meaning of *esse* as essence, but he himself does not ordinarily use *esse* in this sense. See *In I Sent.*, d. 33, q. 1, a. 1, ad 1, ed. Mandonnet, I, p. 766; *In III Sent.*, d. 6, q. 2, a. 2, ed. Moos, III, p. 238.

himself reserved the term *esse* to mean the act of existing. Essence, however, is defined in chapter one in reference to being; it is, St. Thomas says, that through which, and in which, that which is has being.[26] In other words, it is the subject of being, or that which possesses being. It is also the formal cause of the being of a thing, giving it its formal determination, as humanity formally specifies the being of man and renders him a *human* being.

Thus St. Thomas' metaphysical language of being is seen to be perfectly coherent. A being (*ens*) is that which has being (*esse*): *ens dicitur quasi esse habens*.[27] The term 'a being' and 'an essence' do not designate two *things*. As St. Thomas says, "...the term 'a being' (*ens*), which is applied to a thing by reason of its being (*esse*), designates the same thing as the term which is applied to it by reason of its essence."[28] There is an undivided unity of being and essence in all existing things, giving to them both their reality and their intelligibility. In the words of Gerald B. Phelan: "The selfsame thing which is and which is known is a composite of elements, the one essential, the other existential, neither of which can *be* or be intelligible without reference to the other but both of which are co-existent and co-intelligible in the unity of the thing... *Things* are known, (not natures or acts of being) and they are known *to be* through their *esse* and to be what they are through their essence."[29]

Up to now we have been concerned with the meaning of

---

[26] Below, § 4, p. 32.

[27] *In XII Metaph.*, lect. 1, § 2419. St. Thomas sometimes uses *ens* to denote only the act of existing without essence. See *In I Sent.*, d. 8, q. 4, a. 2, ad 2, ed. Mandonnet, I, p. 223; *In IV Metaph.*, lect. 2, § 556. See J. Owens, *ibid.*, pp. 2-10. This use of the term *ens* does not occur in the present treatise.

[28] *In IV Metaph.*, lect. 2, § 558.

[29] Gerald B. Phelan, "The Existentialism of St. Thomas," *G. B. Phelan: Selected Papers*, p. 81.

the term 'a being' as designating an existing thing, endowed with an essence and exercizing the act of existing. In chapter one St. Thomas clarifies a second meaning of the term. Some things are called beings even though they do not have an essence or have being in reality, but only in the mind. In this sense 'nothing' or 'blindness' can be called a being, for it is a term or concept about which we can make intelligible statements. A being in this sense is not a real entity, but a being produced by the mind in its act of asserting a predicate of a subject, as when we say 'blindness is in the eye'. The being signified by the copula 'is' is the union effected by the mind between the subject and predicate. This being is also the truth of the proposition, for when we say 'blindness *is* in the eye' we mean that this assertion is true. Being, in this sense, can be attributed to anything about which we can form an affirmative proposition or say anything true, whether it is an actually existing thing or a privation or negation of being.

Properly speaking, being (*esse*) belongs only to those things that are truly beings (*entia*), namely substances or subsistent things. Being can be attributed to non-subsistent items, such as accidents, forms, and parts, but strictly speaking these do not have being; being is ascribed to them because through them or because of them substances have being in some special way, as for example a man is wise through the quality of wisdom.

The notion of *esse* does not emerge very clearly from St. Thomas' analysis of metaphysical terms in chapter one. The word appears several times in its technical sense, but it is left unexplained. Attention is focused on the notion of *ens* ('a being'), from whose analysis the notion of essence is then disengaged as that in which and through which a thing possesses being (*esse*); but what is the *esse* a thing possesses?

Later chapters make it clear that *esse* is an actuality
received by a thing's essence, which in turn is potential to it.
It is outside the definition of the essence and it forms a
composition with the essence. In God, *esse* is his essence;
he does not possess *esse* but is *esse* itself.[30] *Esse*, understood
purely and simply, contains all perfections. Thus as we
read *On Being and Essence* we come to realize that its most
important term is *esse*. A being is a being only because it
has *esse*; an essence is an essence only through the *esse* that
posits it in reality. But what is *esse*? This is the question
that plagues the reader throughout the treatise and for
which no clear answer is given. But at least we are told the
direction in which to look: the mystery of being (*esse*) is
identical with the mystery of God; if we knew what *esse* is,
we would know the essence of God, for only in him is *esse*
an essence or nature. In creatures *esse* does not have the
status of an essence; they have essences which are other
than *esse* and which exist by participating in the divine
esse.

The identification of God with pure *esse* warns us that
for St. Thomas being is not the mere fact that a thing exists,
or its presence in the world. If this were the meaning of
esse, it would hardly make sense to call God *esse tantum*:
nothing but being, or pure being. In fact, *esse* is dynamic
and energizing act, as Gerald B. Phelan well describes it:
"Things which 'have being' are not 'just there' (Dasein)
like lumps of static essence, inert, immovable, unprogressive
and unchanging. The act of existence (*esse*) is not a state,
it is an act, the act of all acts, and, therefore, must be understood as act and not as any static and definable object of

---

[30] Chapter 4, § 6-7, pp. 55-56.

conception. *Esse* is dynamic impulse, energy, act — the first, the most persistent and enduring of all dynamisms, all energies, all acts. In all things on earth the act of being (*esse*) is the consubstantial urge of nature, a restless, striving force, carrying each being (*ens*) onward, from within the depths of its own reality to its full selfachievement, i.e., fully to be what by its nature it is apt to become."[31]

A large part of the treatise concerns the meaning of essence as it is found on the various levels of reality: in substances composed of form and matter (chapter two), in spiritual substances, i.e. human souls, angels, and God (chapter four), and in accidents (chapter six). The relation of essence to the logical notions of genus, species, and difference occupies chapter three. Chapter five summarizes and develops the findings of the previous three chapters.

As in chapter one, the method employed throughout these chapters is analytic and expository. There are occasional demonstrations, as when the immateriality of separate substances is proved by their power of understanding.[32] But no attempt is made to demonstrate the existence of immaterial substances or the other members of the hierarchy of reality. Whatever reasonings the treatise contains are meant to subserve its main purpose, which is to clarify the meaning of being and essence. St. Thomas is content to sketch the map of reality as it appeared to a Christian philosopher of the thirteenth century, showing how the key notions he has elucidated in chapter one are realized in its different parts.

Some Thomists find an exception to this in chapter four. Here, they believe, St. Thomas proves the existence of God,

---

[31] G. B. Phelan: *Selected Papers*, p. 77.
[32] Chapter 4, § 1, p. 52.

beginning with a demonstration of the distinction between essence and existence in creatures. Indeed, Fr. Gillet claims that this is St. Thomas' most direct and profound proof of God's existence, preferable even to the five ways of the *Summa Theologiae* because it is based on the essences of things, whereas the five ways are founded on their movement and other activities.[33] This chapter has occasioned so much controversy that a word must be said about it.

The purpose of the chapter, stated in its opening sentence, is to clarify the meaning of essence as it found in immaterial substances: human souls, angels, and God. The first point St. Thomas makes is that the essence of human souls and angels, unlike that of material substances, does not include matter but only form. This contradicted the opinion of most of his contemporaries, who followed the Spanish philosopher Avicebron in holding that spiritual substances were composed of form and matter, though their matter was thought to be spiritual and non-quantitative. A composition of form and matter, they thought, was essential to every creature; God alone was incomposite and purely actual.

St. Thomas agreed with his contemporaries that all creatures are composite beings, containing an element of potentiality, but he could not accept a composition of form and matter in spiritual substances, for he regarded the notion

---

[33] See St. M. Gillet, *Thomas d'Aquin* (Paris, 1949), pp. 67-68. Others who consider this to be a proof for God's existence are Fernand Van Steenberghen, "Le problème de l'existence de Dieu dans le 'De ente et essentia' de Saint Thomas d'Aquin," *Mélanges Joseph de Ghellinck*, II (Louvain, 1951), pp. 837-847; J. Owens, *An Elementary Christian Metaphysics* (Milwaukee, 1963), pp. 80-81, 337-338; "Quiddity and Real Distinction in St. Thomas Aquinas," *Mediaeval Studies*, 27 (1965), p. 17. On the contrary, Etienne Gilson denies that it is, properly speaking, a demonstration of God's existence. See his "La preuve du De ente et essentia," *Acta III Congressus Thomistici Internationalis: Doctor Communis*, 3 (Turin, 1950), pp. 257-260; "Trois leçons sur le problème de l'existence de Dieu," *Divinitas*, I (1961), pp. 6-8.

of spiritual matter to be a contradiction in terms. According to him, these substances are composed of essence and being (*esse*), which are related to each other as potency to act.

This is established by a general proof that the essence of every substance except God is distinct from its existence. The proof rests on the fact that existence is not included in the notion of an essence or quiddity. For example, we can form a notion of what a man or phoenix is without knowing whether or not it exists in reality. Being or existence is not contained in the definition of their essence. The only possible exception to this general rule would be a being whose essence is existence itself. Clearly the notion of what this unique being is would contain existence. But the essence or quiddity of every other being can be conceived without including existence in its concept. And since existence is not contained in the notion of its essence, it must come from outside the essence and enter into composition with it. All substances except God, therefore, are composed of essence and existence.[34]

Thomists are far from agreeing on the purpose and nature of this argument.[35] Does it establish anything more than that what a thing is and the fact that it exists are not the

---

[34] Chapter 4, § 6, pp. 55-56.

[35] For the nature of this proof, see J. Owens, "Quiddity and Real Distinction in St. Thomas Aquinas," *Mediaeval Studies*, 27 (1965), pp. 1-22. Cornelio Fabro calls the proof logical in character. See his *La Nozione Metafisica di Partecipazione*, 2nd ed. (Turin, 1950), pp. 218-219. However, as J. Owens points out, the terms of the proof are not logical but metaphysical; they are first, and not second, intentions. See J. Owens, "Quiddity and Real Distinction in St. Thomas," pp. 2-4. Umberto degl' Innocenti, among others, defends the proof as establishing a real distinction. See his "La distinzione reale nel 'De ente et essentia' di S. Tommaso," *Doctor Communis*, 10 (1957), pp. 165-173. Joseph Bobik claims that it establishes a real, ontological otherness of essence and existence. See his *Aquinas On Being and Essence: a Translation and Interpretation* (Notre Dame, Indiana, 1965), pp. 167-170.

same ? Did St. Thomas intend to prove a *real* composition
of essence and existence as two ontological components of
created being, or only a conceptual or logical distinction
between these terms ? The present treatise does not answer
these questions clearly. In other writings St. Thomas explicitly
teaches that there is a real composition of essence and *esse* in
created substances. These two intrinsic principles of a
creature are said to be really distinct.[36] But here he does not
specify the kind of distinction established by this argument.

A clue to St. Thomas' mind on this topic is found in his
Scripta on the *Sentences*, book one, which dates from the
same period as the present treatise. Wishing to show that
being is accidental to a created essence, he points out that
it does not belong to the notion of that essence. For example,
we can understand what human nature is and nonetheless
doubt whether any man actually exists. In the same way
rational is accidental to animal, for rational is not contained
in the definition of animal.[37] Now, St. Thomas clearly does
not mean that the specific difference 'rational' is really
distinct from the genus 'animal'. A conceptual distinction
suffices to account for the accidental relation between them.
On this basis it appears that a conceptual distinction ade-
quately explains the fact that existence is not contained in
the notion of a created essence.

In chapter three there is a similar proof for the distinction
between an individual and its specific nature. When an
essence like humanity is considered in itself or absolutely,

---

[36] See St. Thomas, *De Veritate*, 27, 1, ad 8; *In I Sent.*, d. 13, q. 1, a. 3, ed.
Mandonnet, I, p. 307. For other early texts of St. Thomas affirming a real
difference between essence and *esse* in creatures, see L. Sweeney, "Existence/
Essence in Thomas Aquinas' Early Writings," *Proceedings of the American
Catholic Philosophical Ass'n*, 37 (1963), pp. 103-104.
[37] *In I Sent.*, d. 8, expos. primae partis textus; ed. Mandonnet, I, p. 209.

it is not restricted to one individual, nor is it conceived as existing in many individuals. Both unity and plurality are outside the concept of humanity, and both can be added to it.[38] But this does not establish a real distinction between the individual and its specific nature. St. Thomas, in fact, holds that these are really identical, and distinct only in our thought.[39] Consequently the similar argument for the distinction between essence and existence proves that there is a conceptual, and not necessarily a real, distinction between them.

One of the direct sources of St. Thomas' distinction between essence and *esse* in this treatise is the *De Trinitate* of William of Auvergne. There can hardly be any doubt that St. Thomas had this book in front of him when he wrote *On Being and Essence*. William of Auvergne begins chapter two of his *De Trinitate* (as St. Thomas begins his own treatise) with a clarification of two meanings of the term 'being'. In one sense, he explains, it means the essence or quiddity of a thing, in another sense it means the thing's existence. Now existence is outside the notion of anything we can think about, whether it be a man or donkey or anything else. The only exception is God: we cannot conceive his essence as non-existent, for in him essence and existence are identical in reality. But a creature's essence and its existence are distinct, because the definition of its essence does not include existence.[40] On this ground, however, William of Auvergne hesitated to assert a *real* distinction between a creature's essence and its existence; they are separable, he says, at least by the mind (*saltem intellectu*).[41] Perhaps we would not

---

[38] Chapter 3, § 2, p. 46.
[39] *Contra Gentiles*, I, 26, § 5; *In VII Metaph.*, lect. 13, § 1571.
[40] William of Auvergne, *De Trinitate*, 2 (Paris, 1674), supplementum, p. 2b.
[41] William of Auvergne, *De Universo*, Ia P. I, c. 3; I, p. 594b. M. D. Roland-

betray St. Thomas' intention if we said that when he adopted this proof in the present treatise he thought that it established at least a conceptual distinction between essence and existence in creatures.

William of Auvergne's second way of elucidating the meaning of being leads to the existence of God as being itself.[42] Everything that exists (his argument runs) is either identical with its existence or distinct from it. If a is distinct from its existence, it owes its existence to something else, which we will call b. We will then argue either in a circle, asserting that a owes its existence to b and b owes its existence to a, or in a series, claiming that a owes its existence to b, b owes its existence to c, and so on. The circular argument is contradictory; for if a is the cause of the existence of b, and b is the cause of the existence of a, in order to cause the other each must exist before existing as the other's effect. Therefore it will be prior to itself and the cause of its own existence. On the other hand, if we argue in a series, this series will go on to infinity; but an infinite series can neither be thought nor expressed in language. In short, it is unthinkable and therefore destructive of philosophy itself. Consequently we must grant the existence of a being whose essence is inseparable from its existence even in thought. This being cannot not exist and it cannot be thought not to exist.

A similar analysis of being in *On Being and Essence* leads St. Thomas to the notion of God as the unique being whose essence is identical with its existence; who is, in short,

Gosselin, however, believes that William of Auvergne held the real distinction. See M. D. Roland-Gosselin, *op. cit.*, p. 163. On this point, see E. Gilson, "La notion d'existence chez Guillaume d'Auvergne," pp. 83-84.
[42] William of Auvergne, *De Trinitate, ibid.*, pp. 2-3.

subsistent being.[43] Unlike William of Auvergne, he does not consider the possibility of two things being the cause of each other's existence. He envisages only the case of a series of causes of existence. If the existence of any being is distinct from, and adventitious to, its essence, it must be caused by something. Now the cause of its existence cannot be the essence itself (at least if we are talking about an efficient cause), for nothing can produce itself or give itself existence. Hence its existence must be caused by something else; and since there cannot be an infinite series of causes, "there must be something that is the cause of being for all things, because it is nothing but being." This primary cause of being, who is being in all its purity, is God. Thus it is evident, St. Thomas concludes, that the intelligences or angels are composed of form and being, and that they owe their being to the primary being, who is God.

Did St. Thomas intend this to be a proof of the existence of God? Thomists are not in agreement on the answer to this question. Some, as we have seen, not only think that it is a demonstration of God's existence but they prefer it to the five ways of the *Summa Theologiae*. Etienne Gilson, on the contrary, denies that it is properly speaking a proof of the existence of God.[44] He points out that neither in the present treatise nor in any of St. Thomas' other writings where the same argument is found it is presented as a proof of the existence of God. Moreover, St. Thomas does not use it when he explicitly proposes to prove the existence of God. It is not one of the five ways of the *Summa Theologiae*, nor is it found in the *Contra Gentiles* among "the arguments by which both philosophers and Catholic teachers have proved

[43] Chapter 4, § 6, 7, pp. 55-57.
[44] See above, note 33.

that God exists."[45] It is hardly plausible that St. Thomas would have omitted this approach to God if he considered it to be a formal demonstration of the existence of God. Indeed, he appears to have intentionally avoided using it for this purpose in his major works.

We can see the reason for this if we examine the starting point of the proofs of the existence of God in the two *Summae*. All of these proofs begin with a sensible datum, such as the fact of movement and order in the universe, not with the metaphysical distinction of finite being into essence and existence. This distinction is not an empirical fact: we do not observe the essence or *esse* of things with our senses as we do their movement, generation, and destruction. Hence the distinction between essence and existence cannot be the starting point of the Thomistic proofs of the existence of God.

Far from being the starting point of these proofs, this distinction is demonstrated after them in the two *Summae*. Having proved the existence of God from sensible data, St. Thomas shows that he is identical with being itself, and as such his being is utterly simple, having no composition, not even the composition of essence and existence. Hence in God essence and *esse* are really the same, whereas in all other beings they are distinct. As creatures, they are not being itself but participate being according to the measure determined by their essence. Their being, therefore, is other than their essence.

Although St. Thomas did not use the present treatise's approach to God as a demonstration of God's existence in his two *Summae*, he did not forget it when he wrote these works. It appears in both *Summae* as a means of proving the

---

[45] *Contra Gentiles*, I, 13, § 1.

identity of essence and *esse* in God.[46] Like the rest of the metaphysical treatise, it too found a place in his later theological syntheses.

This interpretation of *On Being and Essence* is in fullest agreement with its stated purpose of explaining the meaning of basic metaphysical terms and with the general tenor of St. Thomas' thought. Of course it is possible that when he wrote the treatise he considered the argument in chapter four to be a valid proof of the existence of God but later set it aside in favor of more suitable demonstrations. But there is no convincing reason for this interpretation. The reasoning in this chapter makes perfectly good sense as a means of clarifying the ontological structure of angelic substances and their relation to God as the primary cause of being, which is the explicit purpose of the chapter.

This translation has been made from the Latin edition of Ludwig Baur. Chapters have been numbered as in the Roland-Gosselin edition. The titles of the chapters appear in some of the older editions and they are found in Baur's critical apparatus. The paragraphing of the text has been changed, and paragraphs have been numbered to facilitate reference to them.

---

[46] *Contra Gentiles*, I, 22, § 6; *Summa Theologiae*, I, 3, 4.

ON BEING AND ESSENCE

PROLOGUE

A slight initial error eventually grows to vast proportions, according to the Philosopher.[1] Now the first conceptions of the intellect are (as Avicenna says)[2] 'a being' and 'an essence'. If, then, we are to avoid mistakes through ignorance of these, we must begin exploring their difficulty by stating what is meant by saying 'a being' and 'an essence', how they are found in different things, and how they are related to the logical notions[3] of genus, species, and difference.

---

[1] Aristotle, *De Coelo*, I, 5, 271b8-13. See St. Thomas, *In I De Coelo et Mundo*, lect. 9, § 4; ed. Leonine, III, p. 38.

[2] Avicenna, *Metaph.*, I, 6 (Venice, 1508), fol. 72rb. The meaning of the primary notions are explained by St. Thomas, *De Veritate*, I, 1. For being as the primary and natural object of the intellect, see *Summa Theologiae*, I, 5, 2; I, 85, 3; I, 87, 3, ad 1; I-II, 94, 2; *Contra Gentiles*, II, 83, § 31; *In I Metaph.*, lect. 2, § 46; *In IV Metaph.*, lect. 6, § 605. See also L. M. Régis, *Epistemology* (New York, 1959), pp. 284-289.

[3] *Intentiones.* The Latin word *intentio* was used by the scholastics to translate the Arabic word for concept. See A. M. Goichon, *Lexique de la Langue Philosophique d'Ibn Sina (Avicenne)*, (Paris, 1938), p. 253, n. 469. For St. Thomas the intentions of logic are not primary, but secondary, intentions. Primary or first intentions are concepts of reality; second intentions are formed by the intellect when it reflects upon itself and the way it understands. They are not concepts of reality, but concepts of concepts. On intentions, see R. Schmidt, *The Domain of Logic according to Saint Thomas Aquinas* (The Hague, 1966); H. D. Simonin, "La notion d'"intentio' dans l'œuvre de S. Thomas d'Aquin," *Revue des Sciences Philosophiques et Théologiques*, 19 (1930), pp. 445-463; A. Hayen, *L'Intentionnel dans la Philosophie de Saint Thomas* (Paris, 1942), pp. 47-53; J. Owens, *An Elementary Christian Metaphysics* (Milwaukee, 1963), pp. 237-241.

Chapter One

THE GENERAL MEANING OF THE TERMS 'A BEING' AND 'AN ESSENCE'

[1] We ought to get our knowledge of simple things from composite things and arrive at what is prior by way of what is posterior, so that the learning process will begin, appropriately, with what is easier. For this reason we must begin with the meaning of 'a being' and proceed to the meaning of 'an essence'.[1]

[2] We must realize (with the Philosopher)[2] that the term 'a being' in itself has two meanings. Taken one way it is divided by the ten categories; taken in the other way it

---

[1] St. Thomas follows Aristotle's rule of learning: begin with what is easier to understand and proceed to what is more difficult. According to Aristotle, we must start with general notions and analyze them into more particular ones. Aristotle says, "Now what is to us plain and obvious at first is rather confused masses, the elements and principles of which become known to us later by analysis." (*Physics*, I, 1, 184a22-24). Although the elements and principles are prior by nature to the composites of which they are parts, they are known after the composites. See Aristotle, *Post. Anal.*, I, 1-2, 71a-72b4; *Metaph.*, VII, 3, 1029b1-7. See also St. Thomas *In VII Metaph.*, lect. 2, § 1300-1305. A being (*ens*) can be analyzed into two principles, essence and being (*esse*). It is thus a composite notion; essence is one of its components, and its notion is disengaged only after we know the meaning of a being.

[2] Aristotle, *Metaph.*, V, 7, 1017a22-35. In the first sense a being is anything in the category of substance or one of the nine accidents; for example, the substance 'man' or the quality 'whiteness'. A being in this sense (*ens per se*) is distinguished from accidental combinations of being, such as 'white man' or 'musical man' (*ens per accidens*). In the second sense a being is a combining of a subject and a predicate in a proposition, such as 'Socrates is musical'. The copula 'is' is the sign of this mode of being, which obviously can exist only in the mind that forms the proposition. The copula 'is' signifies that the proposition is true; hence this mode of being signifies the truth of a proposition. See St. Thomas, *In V Metaph.*, lect. 9; *In X Metaph.*, lect. 3, § 1982; *Quodl.*, II, 3; IX, 3.

signifies the truth of propositions. The difference between the two is that in the second sense anything can be called a being if an affirmative proposition can be formed about it, even though it is nothing positive in reality. In this way privations and negations are called beings, for we say that affirmation *is* opposed to negation, and that blindness *is* in the eye. But in the first way nothing can be called a being unless it is something positive in reality. In the first sense, then, blindness and the like are not beings.[3]

[3] The term 'an essence' is not derived from this second meaning of 'a being', for in this sense some things are called beings that do not have an essence, as is clear in the case of privations. Rather, 'an essence' is derived from 'a being' in the first meaning of the term. As the Commentator says,[4] a being in the first sense of the term is that which signifies the essence of a thing. And because, as we have said,[5] 'a being' in this sense is divided by the ten categories, essence must mean something common to all the natures through which different beings are placed in different genera and species, as for example humanity is the essence of man, and so with regard to other things.

---

[3] This does not mean that evils, such as blindness, are unreal and are not found in reality but only in the mind, as William Barrett interprets this passage in his *Irrational Man* (New York: Anchor Books, 1962), p. 288. Evil is found in things, St. Thomas says, as the lack of a good they should have. As a privation or absence of a good, evil is not a thing or being, with an essence or *esse*. However, when we think of it we conceive it as though it were a being and thus give it the status of a being in our thought. See St. Thomas, *Summa Theologiae*, I, 48, 2; *Contra Gentiles*, III, 7, 8, 9; *De Malo*, I, 1; *In I Sent.*, d. 46, q. 1, a. 2, ad 1, ed. Mandonnet, I, p. 1054. Privations are far from lacking existential import; hell itself, according to St. Thomas, is the privation of grace and of the vision of God. See *In III Sent.*, d. 22, q. 2, a. 1, sol. 2; ed. Moos, III, p. 670.

[4] Averroes, *In V Metaph.*, t. c. 14, fol. 55va56.

[5] See above, § 2.

[4] Because the definition telling what a thing is signifies that by which a thing is located in its genus or species, philosophers have substituted the term 'quiddity' for the term 'essence'. The Philosopher frequently calls this 'what something was to be';[6] that is to say, that which makes a thing to be what it is. It is also called 'form',[7] because form signifies the determination[8] of each thing, as Avicenna says.[9] Another term used for this is 'nature', using 'nature' in the first of the four senses enumerated by Boethius.[10] In this sense anything is called a nature which the intellect can grasp in any way; for a thing is intelligible only through its definition and essence. That is why the Philosopher, too,

---

[6] *Quod quid erat esse.* A literal translation of Aristotle's τὸ τί ἦν εἶναι. This is the 'whatness' of a thing: the answer to the question "What is it essentially and necessarily?" From the point of view of logic this is the complete specific definition; from the point of view of metaphysics it is the formal, intelligible perfection of the thing as opposed to its unintelligible matter. For Aristotle, form is the fundamental being of a thing. There is no adequate English translation of this Aristotelian term. W. D. Ross suggests 'what a thing was to be'; J. Owens, 'what-IS-Being', the capitalized IS expressing the timeless being of the form. See W. D. Ross, *Aristotle's Metaphysics* (Oxford, 1924), I, p. 127; J. Owens, *The Doctrine of Being in the Aristotelian Metaphysics*, 2nd ed. (Toronto, 1963), pp. 180-188. See St. Thomas, *In VII Metaph.*, lect. 5.

[7] Form, in this context, is the whole nature or essence of a thing; it is not the substantial form which, with matter, makes up a material substance. These two meanings of form are called respectively 'form of the whole' (*forma totius*) and 'form of the part' (*forma partis*). The former is the whole essence, including, in the case of a material substance, both substantial form and matter; e.g. humanity. The latter is a part of the essence, uniting with matter to make up the complete essence of a material thing; e.g. the soul of a living being. See below, ch. 2, § 12, pp. 43-44.

[8] *Certitudo.* The Arabic term which the mediaeval translator rendered by this Latin word has the meaning of perfection or complete determination. On the one hand it signifies the objective truth of a thing, on the other the precise and clear knowledge of it. See A. M. Goichon, *La Distinction de l'Essence et de l'Existence d'après Ibn Sina (Avicenne)*, (Paris, 1937), p. 34, n. 7.

[9] Avicenna, *Metaph.*, II, 2, fol. 76ra. See I, 6, fol. 72ra; III, 5, fol. 80rb.

[10] Boethius, *Liber de Persona et Duabus Naturis*, 1; PL 64, 1341BC. See below, note 12.

says that every substance is a nature.[11] The term 'nature'[12] in this sense seems to mean the essence of a thing as directed to its specific operation, for no reality lacks its specific operation. The term 'quiddity' is derived from what is signified by the definition, while 'essence'[13] is used because through it, and in it, that which is has being.[14]

[5] Because we use the term 'a being' absolutely and

---

[11] Aristotle, *Metaph.*, V, 4, 1014b35.

[12] *Natura.* Etymologically, the Latin word *natura*, like the Greek equivalent φύσις and the English 'nature', means 'birth'. St. Thomas says that the word 'nature' first meant the birth of living things, then the inner active principle of that birth, then any intrinsic principle of change or movement. Thus the intrinsic principles of matter and form came to be called 'nature'. Finally the specific essence of a thing, expressed by its definition, was called nature because it is the terminus of generation. See St. Thomas, *Summa Theologiae*, III, 2, 1.

[13] The Latin word *essentia* is derived from the infinitive *esse*, which means 'to be'. Thus the etymology of *essentia* connects it with being. According to St. Thomas, essence is the same as nature or quiddity, but conceived as a potentiality to being. "I call essence that whose actuality is being" (*In I Sent.*, d. 23, q. 1, a. 1; ed. Mandonnet, I, p. 555).

Conceived by abstraction, the essence is identical with the thing that exists; e.g. man. Conceived by precision, the essence is the formal principle of the thing; e.g. humanity. For the distinction between these two ways of conceiving an essence, see J. Owens, *An Elementary Christian Metaphysics* (Milwaukee, 1963), pp. 132-133. See St. Thomas, *Contra Gentiles*, I, 21, §5.

[14] This does not mean that the essence confers being on the substance but that it is in and by means of the essence that the substance receives being. See E. Gilson, *The Christian Philosophy of St. Thomas Aquinas* (New York, 1956), p. 448, n. 30.

A being (*ens*) is that which exists or possesses being (*esse*). See St. Thomas, *In XII Metaph.*, lect. 1, §2419. Being (*esse*) is the actuality that makes a thing a being. *Esse* is the act of being (*actus essendi*). The *esse* of a thing is its supreme perfection, for without it the thing would be nothing. It is the "actuality of all actualities and the perfection of all perfections." (*De Potentia*, VII, 2, ad 9). The existential act that is being is "that which is innermost in everything and most deeply set in all things, because it is formal with respect to everything found in a thing." (*Summa Theologiae*, I, 8, 1). See E. Gilson, *Elements of Christian Philosophy* (New York, 1960), pp. 113-114, 118-119, 178, 189-191, *The Christian Philosophy of St. Thomas Aquinas* (New York, 1956), pp. 29-45; G. B. Phelan: *Selected Papers* (Toronto, 1967), pp. 41-94; J. Owens, *An Elementary Christian Metaphysics*, pp. 60-62.

primarily of substances,[15] and secondarily and with qualification of accidents, it follows that essence is in substances truly and properly, but in accidents in a restricted way and in a qualified sense.

[6] Furthermore, some substances are simple and some composite,[16] and essence is in both; but it is present in simple substances more truly and perfectly because they also have being more perfectly. Simple substances are also the cause of those that are composite; at least this is true of the primary and simple substance, which is God. But because the essences of these substances are to a greater degree hidden from us, we must start with the essences of composite substances, so that the learning process will begin, appropriately, with what is easier.

[15] A substance is "a thing to which it belongs to exist not in a subject"; "that which has a quiddity to which it belongs to exist not in another" (*Contra Gentiles*, I, 25, §10). A substance is a thing or essence that can exist through itself, unlike an accident, that can exist only in a substance as in a subject. It is that which properly speaking exists or possesses being. Since God *is* being itself (*ipsum esse*) and does not possess being, he is not strictly a substance. (*Contra Gentiles*, I, 25). For the distinction between substance, subsistence, person, and essence, see *In I Sent.*, d. 23, q. 1, a. 1; ed. Mandonnet, pp. 553-557. See also E. Gilson, *The Christian Philosophy of St. Thomas Aquinas*, pp. 30-36.

[16] For the distinction between simple or immaterial substances and substances composed of matter and form, see St. Thomas, *De Substantiis Separatis*. St. Thomas, following Aristotle, treats of sensible substances in his commentary on the *Metaphysics*, Book VII, and immaterial substances in Book XI.

Chapter Two

Essence as Found in Composite Substances

[1] Form and matter are found in composite substances, as for example soul and body in man. But it cannot be said that either one of these alone is called the essence. That the matter alone of a thing is not its essence is evident, for through its essence a thing is knowable and fixed in its species and genus. But matter is not a principle of knowledge, and a thing is not placed in a genus or species through it but through that by which a thing is actual.[1] Neither can the form alone of a composite substance be called its essence, though some want to assert this.[2] It is evident from what has been said that the essence is what is signified through the definition of a thing.[3] Now the definition of natural substances includes not only form but also matter; otherwise there would be no difference between definitions in physics and in mathematics.[4] Nor can it be said that the definition

[1] Matter in this context is the primary matter that combines with substantial form to constitute a sensible substance. In itself it is not actually something or knowable. It is the pure possibility of receiving form. Form, on the other hand, is the actuality of matter, making matter actually something and determining it to a genus and species. See St. Thomas, *In VII Metaph.*, lect. 2, § 1285; *In VIII Metaph.*, lect. 1, § 1687.

[2] St. Thomas attributes this opinion to Averroes and some of his followers, while he himself adopts Avicenna's position on this subject. See *In VII Metaph.*, lect. 9, § 1467. On this point, see A. Maurer, "Form and Essence in the Philosophy of St. Thomas," *Mediaeval Studies*, 13 (1951), pp. 165-176.

[3] See above, ch. 1, § 4, pp. 31-32.

[4] In the definition of mathematical entities there is intelligible, but not sensible, matter. For the notion of intelligible matter, see *Summa Theologiae*, I, 85, 1, ad 3; *In Boeth. de Trin.*, V, 3; ed. B. Decker, pp. 184, lines 17-18, p. 186, line 10; *In VII Metaph.*, lect. 10, § 1496, lect. 11, § 1508; *In VIII Metaph.*, lect. 5, § 1760.

of a natural substance includes matter as something added to its essence, or as something outside its essence. This is the kind of definition proper to accidents; not having a perfect essence, their definition must include their subject, which is outside their genus. It is evident, therefore, that essence embraces both matter and form.

[2] Neither can it be said that essence signifies the relation between matter and form, or something added to them, because this would necessarily be accidental or not belonging to the thing, nor could the thing be known through it, both of which are characteristics of essence. For through form, which actualizes matter, matter becomes an actual being and this particular thing. Anything that comes after that does not give matter its basic actual being, but rather a certain kind of actual being, as accidents do, whiteness for example making something actually white. When a form of this kind is acquired, we say that something comes into being not purely and simply but in a certain respect.

[3] It remains, then, that in the case of composite substances the term 'an essence' signifies the composite of matter and form. Boethius agrees with this in his commentary on the *Categories*, where he says that οὐσία signifies the composite;[5] for οὐσία in Greek means the same as our *essentia*, as Boethius himself observes.[6] Furthermore, Avicenna remarks that the quiddity of composite substances is the composition itself of form and matter.[7] The Commentator,

---

[5] Boethius, *In Cat. I, de substantia*; PL 64, 184A. The statement has not been found in Boethius' works. See M. D. Roland-Gosselin, *Le "De Ente et Essentia" de S. Thomas d'Aquin* (Paris, 1948), p. 8, n. 1.

[6] Boethius, *Liber de Persona et Duabus Naturis*, 3; PL 64, 1344CD.

[7] Avicenna, *Metaph.*, V, 5, fol. 90ra.

too, says, "The nature that species have in things subject to generation is something intermediate, a composite of matter and form." [8] This is reasonable, too, for the being that a composite substance has is not the being of the form alone nor of the matter alone but of the composite, and it is essence according to which a thing is said to be. [9] So the essence, according to which a thing is called a being, cannot be either the form alone or the matter alone, but both, though form alone is in its own way the cause of this being. We observe in the case of other things composed of several principles that they do not take their name from one of these principles alone, but from both together. This is clear in tastes. Sweetness is caused by the action of the hot dissolving the moist; and although in this way heat is the cause of sweetness, a body is not called sweet from its heat but from its taste, which includes the hot and the moist. [10]

[4] Because matter is the principle of individuation, it might seem to follow that an essence, which embraces in itself both matter and form, is only particular and not universal. If this were true, it would follow that universals could not be defined, granted that essence is what is signified by the definition. What we must realize is that the matter which is the principle of individuation is not just any matter,

---

[8] Averroes, *In VII Metaph.*, t. c. 27, fol. 83va41.

[9] A thing is said to be according to its essence because it receives its being in and through the essence. See above, ch. 1, § 4, p. 32. An essence formally determines and limits being or existential act. See J. Owens, *An Elementary Christian Metaphysics* (Milwaukee, 1963), pp. 147-148.

[10] See St. Thomas, *In I Sent.*, d. 23, q. 1, a. 1; ed. Mandonnet, I, p. 555. This is the Aristotelian theory of taste. See Aristotle, *De Sensu*, 4, 440 b 30-442 a 17; St. Thomas, *In De Sensu et Sensato*, lect. 10; *Opera Omnia* (New York, 1949), 20, p. 171.

but only designated matter.[11] By designated matter I mean that which is considered under determined dimensions.[12] This kind of matter is not part of the definition of man as man, but it would enter into the definition of Socrates if Socrates could be defined. The definition of man, on the contrary, does include undesignated matter. In this definition we do not put this particular bone and this particular flesh, but bone and flesh absolutely, which are the undesignated matter of man.

[5] It is clear, therefore, that the difference between the essence of Socrates and the essence of man lies solely in what is designated and not designated. This is why the Commentator says, "Socrates is nothing else than animality and rationality, which are his quiddity."[13] The essence of the

---

[11] A thing is said to be designated (*designatum, signatum*) when it can be shown or pointed to with the finger. This is true of the individual thing but not of the abstract nature or essence. The latter can be defined; the former cannot be defined but it can only be pointed to. In this sense, 'designated' is equivalent to the demonstrative article 'this'. A derived meaning of the word is 'determined' or 'limited'. The undesignated is the undetermined, confused, undifferentiated. St. Thomas owes this language to Boethius and the Latin translation of Avicenna. See M. D. Roland-Gosselin, *op. cit.*, p. 11, n. 1; pp. 58-60.

[12] St. Thomas always maintained that matter and its quantitative dimensions account for the existence of many individuals in the same species. In the present work he says that the dimensions are *determined,* following the opinion of Avicenna. In other works, written shortly after *On Being and Essence,* he uses the Averroist notion of *undetermined* dimensions to account for individuation. See *In II Sent.*, d. 3, q. 1, a. 4; ed. Mandonnet, II, p. 97; *In Boet. de Trin.*, IV, 2, ad 3; ed. B. Decker, p. 144. On this subject, see M. D. Roland-Gosselin, *op. cit.*, pp. 106-117.

According to St. Thomas there is a reciprocal causality of matter and form, both of which play a role in the individuation of sensible substance. Matter plays the passive role, making possible the multiplication of form in many individuals. But matter itself exists only through form, and both exist only through the act of existing that posits the substance in the real world. See E. Gilson, *The Christian Philosophy of St. Thomas Aquinas* (New York, 1956), p. 470, n. 10.

[13] Averroes, *In VII Metaph.*, t. c. 20, fol. 80ra23.

genus and the essence of the species also differ as designated and undesignated, though the mode of designation is different in the two cases. The individual is designated with respect to its species through matter determined by dimensions, whereas the species is designated with respect to the genus through the constitutive difference, which is derived from the form of the thing. This determination or designation which is in a species with regard to its genus is not caused by something existing in the essence of the species and in no way in the essence of the genus; rather, whatever is in the species is also in the genus but in an undetermined way. If indeed 'animal' were not wholly what 'man' is, but only a part of him, 'animal' could not be predicated of 'man', since no integral part may be predicated of its whole.

[6]   We can see how this comes about if we examine the difference between body when it means a part of animal and body when it means a genus; for it cannot be a genus in the same way that it is an integral part. In short, the term 'body' can have several meanings.[14] In the genus of substance we give the name 'body' to that which has a nature such that three dimensions can be counted in it; but these three determined dimensions themselves are a body in the genus of quantity. It does happen that something having one perfection may also possess a further perfection, as is evident in man, who has a sensitive nature and, besides this, an intellectual nature. So, too, over and above the perfection of having a form such that three dimensions can be designated in it, another perfection can be added, such as

---

[14] For the distinction between these two meanings of 'body', see *Summa Theologiae*, I, 7, 3; I, 18, 2; *In III Metaph.*, lect. 13, § 514; *In VII Metaph.*, lect. 12, § 1547; *In X Metaph.*, lect. 4, § 1993. See also J. Owens, *op. cit.*, pp. 319-320.

life, or something of the kind. The term 'body', therefore, can signify that which has such a form as allows the determination of three dimensions in it, prescinding[15] from everything else, so that from that form no further perfection may follow. If anything else is added, it will be outside the meaning of body thus understood. In this way body will be an integral and material part of a living being, because the soul will be outside what is signified by the term 'body' and will be joined to this body in such a way that a living being is made up of these two, body and soul, as of two parts.

[7] The term 'body' can also be taken to mean a thing having a form such that three dimensions can be counted in it, no matter what that form may be, whether some further perfection can be derived from it or not. In this sense of the term, body is the genus of animal, because animal does not include anything that is not implicitly contained in body. The soul is not a form different from that which gives to the thing three determined dimensions. That is why, when we said that a body is that which has such a form as allows the determination of three dimensions in it, we understood this to mean any form whatsoever: animality, stoneness, or any other form. In this way the form of animal is implicitly contained in the form of body, inasmuch as body is its genus. And such also is the relation of animal to man. If

---

[15] *Praecisio.* A word occurring several times in this and subsequent chapters. (See ch. 2 § 11, 12; ch. 3, §4; ch. 5, §2). Precision is a mode of abstraction by which we cut off or exclude something from a notion. Abstraction is the consideration of something without either including or excluding from its notion characteristics joined to it in reality. Abstraction without precision does not exclude anything from which it abstracts, but includes the whole thing, though implicitly and indeterminately. See F. A. Blanche, "L'Abstraction," *Mélanges Thomistes* (*Bibliothèque Thomiste*, III, Le Saulchoir, Kain, Belgium, 1923), pp. 237-251; J. Owens, *op. cit.*, pp. 63-64, 132.

'animal' designated only a certain reality endowed with a perfection such that it could sense and be moved through an internal principle, prescinding from any other perfection, then any further perfection would be related to animal as a part and not as implicitly contained in the notion of animal, and then animal would not be a genus. But it is a genus when it signifies a thing whose form can be the source of sensation and movement, no matter what that form may be, whether it be only a sensitive soul or a soul that is both sensitive and rational.

[8] The genus, then, signifies indeterminately everything in the species and not the matter alone. Similarly, the difference designates the whole and not the form alone, and the definition also signifies the whole, as does the species too, though in a different way. The genus signifies the whole as a name designating what is material in the thing without the determination of the specific form. Thus the genus is taken from matter, though it is not matter, as we can clearly see from the fact that we call a body that which has a perfection such that it is determined by three dimensions, a perfection that is related as material with respect to a further perfection. On the contrary, the difference is a term taken from a definite form in a precise way, without including a definite matter in its primary notion; as for example when we say 'animated' (in other words, what has a soul) we do not specify what the thing is, whether it is a body or something else. That is why Avicenna says that the genus is not conceived in the difference as a part of its essence, but only as something outside its essence, as the subject is contained in the notion of its properties.[16] That is also why, according to

---

[16] Avicenna, *Metaph.*, V, 6, fol. 90va.

the Philosopher,[17] a genus is not predicated of a difference
properly speaking, except perhaps as a subject is predicated of
its property. As for the definition or species, it embraces
both, namely the determinate matter signified by the name
of the genus, and the determinate form signified by the name
of the difference.

[9]   From this it is clear why genus, species, and difference
are related proportionately to matter, form, and composite
in nature, though they are not identical with them. A genus
is not matter, but it is taken from matter as designating the
whole; and a difference is not form, but it is taken from form
as designating the whole. That is why we say that man is a
rational animal, and not that he is composed of animal and
rational, as we say that he is composed of soul and body.
We say that man is a being composed of soul and body as
from two things there is constituted a third entity which
is neither one of them: man indeed is neither soul nor body.
If in a sense we may say that man is composed of animal and
rational, it will not be as a third reality is made up of two
other realities, but as a third concept is formed from two other
concepts. The concept 'animal' signifies the nature of a
being without the determination of its special form, containing only what is material in it with respect to its ultimate
perfection. The concept of the difference 'rational', on the
other hand, contains the determination of the special form.
From these two concepts is formed the concept of the species
or definition. This is why, just as a reality composed of
several things cannot be the subject of attribution of its
constituent elements, neither can a concept be the subject

[17] Aristotle, *Metaph.*, III, 3, 998b24; *Topics*, IV, 2, 122b20.

of attribution of the concepts from which it is formed: we do not say that the definition is the genus or difference.

[10]   Although the genus signifies the whole essence of the species, it is not necessary that different species of the same genus have one essence. The unity of the genus comes from its indetermination or indifference, but not in such a way that what is signified by the genus is a nature numerically the same in different species, to which would be added something else (the difference) determining it as a form determines a matter that is numerically one. Rather, the genus denotes a form (though not precisely any one in particular) which the difference expresses in a definite way, and which is the same as that which the genus denotes in-determinately. That is why the Commentator asserts[18] that primary matter is said to be one because of the elimi-nation of all forms, whereas a genus is said to be one because of the community of the designated form. It is clear, therefore, that when the indetermination which caused the unity of the genus is removed by the addition of the difference, there remain species different in essence.

[11]   As we have said,[19] the nature of the species is inde-terminate with regard to the individual, as the nature of the genus with regard to the species. It follows that, just as the genus, when attributed to the species, implies indistinctly in its signification everything that is in the species in a determinate way, so the species, when attributed to the individual, must signify everything essentially in the indi-vidual, though in an indistinct way. For example, the term

---

[18] Averroes, *In XII Metaph.*, t. c. 14, fol. 141va53-b18.
[19] See above, § 5, pp. 37-38.

'man' signifies the essence of the species, and therefore 'man' is predicated of Socrates. But if the nature of the species is signified with precision from designated matter, which is the principle of individuation, then it will have the role of a part. This is the way it is signified by the term 'humanity', for humanity signifies that by which man is man. Now designated matter does not make man to be man, and thus it is not in any way included among the factors that make man to be man. Since, therefore, the concept of humanity includes only that which makes man to be man, its meaning clearly excludes or prescinds from designated matter; and because the part is not predicated of the whole, humanity is predicated neither of man nor of Socrates. Avicenna concludes[20] from this that the quiddity of a composite is not the composite itself whose quiddity it is, though the quiddity itself is a composite. For example, although humanity is a composite, it is not man; in fact, it must be received in something else, namely designated matter.

[12]   As was said above,[21] the species is determined relative to the genus through form, while the individual is determined relative to the species through matter. That is why it is necessary that the term signifying that from which the nature of the genus is derived, prescinding from the determinate form completing the species, signify the material part of the whole, as for example the body is the material part of man. On the contrary, the term signifying that from which the nature of the species is derived, prescinding from designated matter, signifies the formal part. For this reason 'humanity' is a term signifying a certain form, called the

---

[20] Avicenna, *Metaph.*, V, 5, fol. 90ra.
[21] See above, § 5, pp. 37-38.

form of the whole.[22] Not indeed that it is something as it were added to the essential parts, form and matter, as the form of a house is added to its integral parts; but it is the form which is the whole, embracing both form and matter, but prescinding from those factors which enable matter to be designated.

[13] It is clear, then, that the essence of man is signified by the two terms 'man' and 'humanity', but in different ways, as we have said.[23] The term 'man' expresses it as a whole, because it does not prescind from the designation of matter but contains it implicitly and indistinctly, as we said the genus contains the difference.[24] That is why the term 'man' can be predicated of individuals. But the term 'humanity' signifies the essence of man as a part, because its meaning includes only what belongs to man as man, prescinding from all designation of matter. As a result it cannot be predicated of individual men. Because of this the term 'essence' is sometimes attributed to a thing and sometimes denied of it: we can say 'Socrates is an essence' and also 'the essence of Socrates is not Socrates'.

---

[22] See above, ch. 1, note 7, p. 31.
[23] See above, §11, p. 43.
[24] See above, §5, p. 38.

Chapter Three

THE RELATION OF ESSENCE TO GENUS, SPECIES,
AND DIFFERENCE

[1]   Having seen what the term 'an essence' means in composite substances, we must examine how it is related to the
notion[1] of genus, species, and difference. That to which the
notion of genus, species, or difference belongs is attributed
to an individual, determinate thing. It is therefore impossible that the notion of universal (that is to say, of genus
or species) should belong to an essence when it is expressed
as a part, for example by the term 'humanity' or 'animality'.
That is why Avicenna says[2] that 'rationality' is not a difference, but the principle of a difference; and for the same
reason 'humanity' is not a species nor 'animality' a genus.
Nor can we say that the notions of genus and species belong
to an essence as a reality existing outside individual things,
as the Platonists held,[3] because then the genus and species
would not be attributed to the individual: we cannot say
that Socrates is something separated from himself. This
separated entity, moreover, would be of no help in knowing
the individual. We conclude, therefore, that the notion of

---

[1] *Ratio.* As used throughout this chapter, this word is synonymous with
intentio (see above, Prologue, note 3). *Ratio* is the intelligible character of
a thing as grasped by the mind; it is what the name of a thing means or
its definition signifies. The *ratio* as understood (*ratio intellecta*) is the concept. See St. Thomas, *In I Sent.*, d. 2, q. 1, a. 3; ed. Mandonnet, I, pp.
66-67; d. 33, q. 1, a. 1, ad 3, p. 767. See also J. Peghaire, *Intellectus et Ratio
selon S. Thomas d'Aquin* (Paris, 1936), pp. 14-15.
[2] Avicenna, *Metaph.*, V, 6, fol. 90rb.
[3] See Aristotle, *Metaph.*, I, 9, 990 b 1 - 991 a 14. See also St. Thomas,
In I Metaph., lect. 14; *Summa Theologiae*, I, 85,1; R. J. Henle, *Saint Thomas
and Platonism* (The Hague, 1956), pp. 333-345.

genus or species applies to an essence when it is expressed as
a whole, for example by the term 'man' or 'animal', containing implicitly and indistinctly everything in the individual.

[2]   Understood in this sense, a nature or essence can be
considered in two ways.[4] First, absolutely, according to its
proper meaning. In this sense nothing is true of it except
what belong to it as such; whatever else may be attributed
to it, the attribution is false. For example, to man as man
belong 'rational', 'animal', and everything else included in
his definition; but 'white' or 'black', or any similar attribute
not included in the notion of humanity, does not belong to
man as man. If someone should ask, then, whether a nature
understood in this way can be called one or many, we should
reply that it is neither, because both are outside the concept
of humanity, and it can happen to be both. If plurality
belonged to its concept, it could never be one, though it is
one when present in Socrates. So, too, if oneness belonged
to its concept, the nature of Socrates and of Plato would be
identical, and it could not be multiplied in many individuals.

[3]   In a second way a nature or essence can be considered
according to the being it has in this or that individual.
In this way something is attributed to it accidentally, because of the subject in which it exists, as we say that man is
white because Socrates is white, though this does not belong
to man insofar as he is man.

---

[4] For the twofold consideration of essence St. Thomas follows Avicenna,
Metaph., V, 1-2, fol. 86va-87v; *Logica*, I, fol. 2b; *De Anima*, II, 2, fol. 6vb.
But unlike Avicenna, St. Thomas does not attribute being to essence ab-
solutely considered. See J. Owens, *An Elementary Christian Metaphysics*
(Milwaukee, 1963), pp. 131-142; "Unity and Essence in St. Thomas
Aquinas," *Mediaeval Studies*, 23 (1961), pp. 240-259.

[4] This nature has a twofold being: one in individual things and the other in the soul, and accidents follow upon the nature because of both beings. In individuals, moreover, the nature has a multiple being corresponding to the diversity of individuals; but none of these beings belongs to the nature from the first point of view, that is to say, when it is considered absolutely. It is false to say that the essence of man as such has being in this individual: if it belonged to man as man to be in this individual it would never exist outside the individual. On the other hand, if it belonged to man as man not to exist in this individual, human nature would never exist in it. It is true to say, however, that it does not belong to man as man to exist in this or that individual, or in the soul. So it is clear that the nature of man, considered absolutely, abstracts from every being, but in such a way that is prescinds from no one of them; and it is the nature considered in this way that we attribute to all individuals.

[5] Nevertheless, it cannot be said that a nature thus considered has the character of a universal,[5] because unity and community are included in the definition of a universal, neither of which belongs to human nature considered absolutely. If community were included in the concept of man, community would be found in everything in which humanity is found. This is false, because there is nothing common in Socrates; everything in him is individuated.[6] Neither can

---

[5] For the notion of a universal, see *Summa Theologiae*, I, 85, 3, ad 1; *In VII Metaph.*, lect. 13, § 1570-1576; *In I Perihermenias*, lect. 10, ed. Leonine, I, pp. 47-51; *In I Post Anal.*, lect. 11, ed. Leonine, I, pp. 179-181. See R. Schmidt, *The Domain of Logic according to Saint Thomas Aquinas* (The Hague, 1966), pp. 177-201.

[6] See *Contra Gentiles*, I, 26, § 5.

it be said that human nature happens to have the character
of a genus or species through the being it has in individuals,
because human nature is not found in individual men as
a unity, as though it were one essence belonging to all of
them, which is required for the notion of a universal.

[6] It remains, then, that human nature happens to have
the character of a species only through the being it has in
the intellect. Human nature has being in the intellect
abstracted from all individuating factors, and thus it has a
uniform character with regard to all individual men outside
the soul, being equally the likeness of all and leading to a
knowledge of all insofar as they are men. Because it has this
relation to all individual men, the intellect discovers the
notion of species and attributes it to the nature. This is
why the Commentator says that it is the intellect that causes
universality in things.[7] Avicenna makes the same point.[8]

[7] Although this nature apprehended by the intellect has
the character of a universal from its relation to things outside the soul, because it is one likeness of them all, nevertheless as it has being in this or that intellect it is a particular
apprehended likeness. The Commentator was clearly in
error then; he wanted to conclude that the intellect is one
in all men from the universality of the apprehended form.[9]
In fact, the universality of this form is not due to the being
it has in the intellect but to its relation to things as their

[7] Averroes, *In I De Anima*, t. c. 8, fol. 109vb23.
[8] Avicenna, *Metaph.*, V, 1, fol. 87rb; 87v. See St. Thomas, *In II Sent.*,
d. 17, q. 2, a. 1, ad 3; ed. Mandonnet, II, p. 429.
[9] Averroes, *ibid.*, III, t. c. 5, fol. 164ra21ff. See St. Thomas, *In II Sent.*,
d. 17, q. 2, a. 1; ed. Mandonnet, II, pp. 420-430; *Summa Theologiae*, I,
76, 1-2; *De Unitate Intellectus contra Averroistas Parisienses*; *Quaest. Disp. De
Anima*, 2, 3; *De Spiritualibus Creaturis*, 9.

likeness. In the same way, if there were a material statue representing many men, the image or likeness of the statue would have its own individual being as it existed in this determinate matter, but it would have the nature of something common as the general representation of many men.

[8]   Because it is human nature absolutely considered that is predicated of Socrates, this nature does not have the character of a species when considered absolutely; this is one of the accidents that accompany it because of the being it has in the intellect. That is why the term 'species' is not predicated of Socrates, as though we were to say 'Socrates is a species'. This would necessarily happen, however, if the notion of species belonged to man in his individual being in Socrates, or according to his absolute consideration, namely insofar as he is man; for we predicate of Socrates everything that belongs to man as man. Nevertheless, it is essential to a genus to be predicated: this is included in its definition. Predication is something achieved by the intellect in its act of combining and dividing, having for its foundation in reality the unity of those things, one of which is attributed to the other.[10] That is why the notion of predicability can be included in the meaning of the notion of genus, a notion that is also produced by an act of the intellect. But that to which the intellect attributes the notion of predicability, combining it

[10] By the act of combining or dividing St. Thomas means the act of affirmative or negative judging. See *In Boeth. De Trinitate*, V, 3; ed. Decker, p. 182; *In I Perihermenias*, lect. 3; ed. Leonine, § 4-5, p. 16. A judgment is a synthesis made by the intellect. If it is a true judgment, it corresponds to the being of things. Thus the truth of judgment is based on the being of things. See G. B. Phelan, "Verum sequitur esse rerum," *Mediaeval Studies*, I (1939), pp. 11-22 (reprinted in *Selected Papers*, pp. 133-154); J. Owens, *op. cit.*, pp. 248-258. For the notion of predication, see R. Schmidt, *op. cit.*, pp. 202-241.

with something else, is not the concept itself of genus, but
rather that to which the intellect attributes the concept of
genus, as for example what is signified by the term 'animal'.

[9]   From this we can see how essence or nature is related
to the notion of species. The notion of species is not one of
those items that belong to the nature when it is considered
absolutely, nor is it one of the accidents that follow upon the
nature because of the being it has outside the soul, like
whiteness or blackness. Rather, the notion of species is one
of the accidents that follow upon the nature because of the
being it has in the intellect; and it is in this way, too, that
the notions of genus and difference belong to it.

Chapter Four

Essence as Found in Separate Substances

[1] It remains for us to see how essence exists in the separate substances: in souls, intelligences,[1] and the first cause. Although everyone admits the simplicity of the first cause, some would like to introduce a composition of form and matter in intelligences and souls,[2] an opinion that seems to have begun with Avicebron, the author of *The Source of Life*.[3] But this is opposed to what philosophers generally say; they call these substances separated from matter and prove

---

[1] By intelligences St. Thomas means angels. See his treatise *De Substantiis Separatis, seu De Angelorum Natura*. It is unusual for him to include human souls among the separate substances. On the nature of angels, see James Collins, *The Thomistic Philosophy of the Angels* (Washington, 1947); Etienne Gilson, *The Christian Philosophy of St. Thomas Aquinas* (New York, 1956), pp. 160-173.

[2] The common doctrine of the Franciscans, with the exception of John of Rupella. See Alexander of Hales (?) *Summa Theologica*, I-II, Inq. II, tr. II, q. unica, n. 106 (Quaracchi, II, p. 135); St. Bonaventure, *In II Sent.*, d. 3, p. 1, a. 1, q. 1 (Quaracchi, II, p. 91); Roger Bacon, *Liber Primus Communium Naturalium*, p. IV, d. 3, c. 4 (*Opera*, Oxford, 1911. Fasc. III, p. 291). It was also taught by some Dominicans, for example by Roland of Cremona, Peter of Tarantasia, Robert Fishacre, Robert Kilwardby, and Gerard of Abbeyville. See O. Lottin, "La composition hylémorphique des substances spirituelles. Les débuts de la controverse," *Revue Néoscolastique de Philosophie*, 34 (1932), pp. 21-41; E. Kleineidam, *Das Problem der hylomorphen Zusammensetzung der geistigen Substanzen im 13. Jahrhundert, behandelt bis Thomas von Aquin* (Breslau, 1930); M. D. Roland-Gosselin, *op. cit.*, p. 30, note 2. See St. Thomas, *Summa Theologiae*, I, 50, 2; *Contra Gentiles*, II, 50-51; *De Substantiis Separatis*, 5, 18; *De Spiritualibus Creaturis*, 1.

[3] Avicebron (Ibn Gebirol), *Fons Vitae*, III, n. 18; ed. C. Baeumker, *Beiträge zur Geschichte der Philosophie des Mittelalters*, I (Münster, 1892), p. 118. Solomon Ibn Gabirol was a Spanish Jew who lived *ca.* 1021-1058. See E. Gilson, *History of Christian Philosophy in the Middle Ages* (New York, 1955), pp. 226-229; M. Wittmann, *Die Stellung des hl. Thomas von Aquin zu Avencebrol (Ibn Gebirol)*, *Beiträge*, III (Münster, 1900).

that they are completely immaterial.[4] This is best demonstrated from their power of understanding.[5] We see that forms are actually intelligible only when they are separated from matter and its conditions ; and they are made actually intelligible only through the power of an intelligent substance, by receiving them into itself and acting upon them.[6] That is why every intellectual substance must be completely free from matter, neither having matter as a part of itself nor being a form impressed on matter, as is the case with material forms.

[2] The position is untenable that not all matter prevents intelligibility but only corporeal matter. If this resulted only from corporeal matter, matter would have this opaqueness to understanding from its corporeal form, since matter is called corporeal only because it exists under a corporeal form. This is impossible, because this corporeal form, like other forms, is actually intelligible insofar as it is abstracted from matter. In a soul or intelligence, therefore, there is no composition of matter and form, understanding matter in them as it is in corporeal substances. But there is in them a composition of form and being.[7] That is why the com-

---

[4] See Aristotle, *De Anima*, III, 4, 429a10-25; St. Albert, *In II Sent.*, d. 1, a. 4; ed. Borgnet, 27, p. 14b.

[5] See Avicenna, *De Anima*, V, 2, fol. 22vb; 23rb; St. Albert, *In II Sent.*, d. 19, a. 1, sed contra 3, p. 329a.

[6] That is, the intellectual being gives to the form an intentional mode of existing within itself. See A. Hayen, *L'Intentionnel dans la Philosophie de Saint Thomas* (Paris, 1942), pp. 47-53; J. Owens, *An Elementary Christian Metaphysics* (Milwaukee, 1963), pp. 31-32.

[7] See *Summa Theologiae*, I, 50, 2, ad 3; *Contra Gentiles*, II, 52-54; *De Spiritualibus Creaturis*, 1. In the *De Veritate*, I, 27, ad 8, this is called a "real composition", and in *In I Sent.*, d. 13, q. 1, a. 3, ed. Mandonnet, I, p. 307 a "real diversity." On the real composition of essence and *esse* in angels and in all creatures, see E. Gilson, *Le Thomisme*, 6th ed. (Paris, 1965), pp. 171-183. (This edition improves on previous ones and on the trans-

mentary on the *Book of Causes* says that an intelligence is that which has form and being;[8] and by form is here understood the quiddity itself or simple nature.

[3] It is easy to see how this is so. Whenever things are so related to each other that one is the cause of the other's being, the one that is the cause can have being without the other, but not vice versa. Now matter and form are so related that form gives being to matter. Matter, then, cannot exist without some form, but there can be a form without matter: form as such does not depend on matter. If we find some forms that can exist only in matter, this happens to them because they are far removed from the first principle, which is the primary and pure act. It follows that those forms closest to the first principle are forms subsisting in themselves without matter. In fact, not every kind of form needs matter, as has been said; and the intelligences are forms of this kind. There is no necessity, then, that the essences or quiddities of these substances be anything else than form.

lation: *The Christian Philosophy of St. Thomas*, pp. 35-40). J. Owens, *op. cit.* pp. 101-106; "Quiddity and Real Distinction in St. Thomas Aquinas," *Mediaeval Studies*, 27 (1965), pp. 1-22; C. Fabro, *La Nozione Metafisica di Partecipazione secondo S. Tommaso D'Aquino*, 3rd ed. (Turin, 1963), pp. 212-244. For the history of the distinction between essence and existence, see M. D. Roland-Gosselin, *op. cit.*, pp. 137-205.

[8] *Liber de Causis*, a Latin translation of a neoplatonic treatise whose contents are taken from Proclus' *Elements of Theology*. See O. Bardenhewer, *Die pseudo-aristotelische Schrift "Ueber das reine Gute" bekannt unter dem Namen "Liber de Causis"* (Freiburg i. Breisgau, 1882), 8, p. 173. St. Thomas was the first to recognize the true source of the treatise. See his *Expositio super Librum de Causis*, ed. H. D. Saffrey, p. 3. St. Thomas accommodates the words of the *Liber de Causis* to his own doctrine: the composition of form and being found in this work is not one between essence and being in the Thomistic sense, but between being, understood as the primary substratum of things and their essential determinations or forms, such as life and intelligence. See M. D. Roland-Gosselin, *op. cit.*, pp. 146-149; St. Thomas, *In Librum de Causis*, 9; ed. H. D. Saffrey, p. 64.

[4] The essence of a composite substance accordingly differs from that of a simple substance because the essence of a composite substance is not only form but embraces both form and matter, whereas the essence of a simple substance is form alone. Two other differences follow from this. The first is that we can signify the essence of a composite substance as a whole or as a part. This happens because of the designation of matter, as has been said.[9] As a result we do not attribute the essence of a composite in every way to the composite; we cannot say, for example, that man is his quiddity. But the essence of a simple reality, which is its form, can only be signified as a whole, because nothing is there beside the form as its recipient. That is why the essence of a simple substance, no matter how we conceive it, can be attributed to the substance. As Avicenna says, "The quiddity of a simple substance is the simple entity itself," because there is nothing else that receives it.[10]

[5] The second difference is that the essences of composite things, by being received in designated matter, are multiplied according as it is divided. From this it happens that there are things the same in species and different in number. But since the essence of a simple entity is not received in matter, it cannot be multiplied in this way. That is why in these substances we cannot find many individuals in the same species; there are as many species among them as there are individuals, as Avicenna expressly says.[11]

[9] See above, ch. 2, § 13, p. 44.
[10] Avicenna, *Metaph.*, V, 5, fol. 90ra. See St. Thomas, *Summa Theologiae*, I, 50, 4; *Contra Gentiles*, II, 93.
[11] Avicenna, *ibid.*, fol. 87va.

[6] Substances of this kind, though pure forms without matter, are not absolutely simple; they are not pure act but have a mixture of potentiality. The following consideration makes this evident. Everything that does not belong to the concept of an essence or quiddity comes to it from outside and enters into composition with the essence, because no essence can be understood without its parts. Now, every essence or quiddity can be understood without knowing anything about its being. I can know, for instance, what a man or a phoenix is and still be ignorant whether it has being in reality.[12] From this it is clear that being is other than essence or quiddity, unless perhaps there is a reality whose quiddity is its being. This reality, moreover, must be unique and primary;[13] because something can be multiplied only [1] by adding a difference (as a generic nature is multiplied in species), [2] by the reception of a form in different parts of matter (as a specific nature is multiplied in different individuals), [3] by the distinction between what is separate and what is received in something (for example, if there were a separated heat,[14] by the fact of its separation it would be distinct from heat that is not separated). Now, granted that there is a reality that is pure

---

[12] This argument for the distinction between essence and being is found in other works of St. Thomas: *In I Sent.*, d. 8, Expositio primae partis textus, ed. Mandonnet, I, p. 209; d. 8, q. 4, a. 3, p. 222; *In II Sent.*, d. 1, q. 1, a. 1, p. 12; d. 3, q. 1, a. 2, p. 87; *De Veritate*, X, 12. See L. Sweeney, "Existence/Essence in Thomas Aquinas's Early Writings," *Proceedings of the American Catholic Philosophical Ass'n*, 37 (1963), pp. 97-131; *A Metaphysics of Authentic Existentialism* (Englewood Cliffs, New Jersey, 1965), pp. 70-71. J. Owens, *op. cit.*, pp. 103-104, note 10. C. Fabro, *op. cit.*, pp. 218-219.

[13] See *De Substantiis Separatis*, 8, § 42; ed. F. Lescoe, p. 79.

[14] A separated heat of this kind would be a subsistent form (heat-in-itself), independent of all hot things and by participating in which all things are hot. St. Thomas, of course, uses this as a hypothetical example without subscribing to the Platonic doctrine of separated forms. For his interpretation of Platonism, see R. Henle, *Saint Thomas and Platonism* (The Hague, 1956), pp. 351-361.

being, so that being itself is subsistent, this being would not receive the addition of a difference, because then it would not be being alone but being with the addition of a form. Much less would it receive the addition of matter, because then it would not be subsistent, but material, being. It follows that there can be only one reality that is identical with its being. In everything else, then, its being must be other than its quiddity, nature, or form. That is why the being of the intelligences must be in addition to their form; as has been said,[15] an intelligence is form and being.

[7] Whatever belongs to a thing is either caused by the principles of its nature (as the capacity for laughter in man) or comes to it from an extrinsic principle (as light in the air from the influence of the sun). Now being itself cannot be caused by the form or quiddity of a thing (by 'caused' I mean by an efficient cause), because that thing would then be its own cause and it would bring itself into being, which is impossible.[16] It follows that everything whose being is distinct from its nature must have being from another. And because everything that exists through another is reduced to that which exists through itself as to its first cause,

[15] See above, § 2, p. 52.

[16] See *Contra Gentiles*, I, 22, § 6. The form is not the efficient, but the formal cause, of being. See J. Owens, *op. cit.*, pp. 76, 147-148. In this sense St. Thomas can say that "the being of composites arises from the components" (*In IX Metaph.*, lect. 11, § 1903); that "being is, as it were, constituted through the principles of essence (i.e. matter and form)" (*In IV Metaph.*, lect. 2, § 558); that the being of a thing "results from the union of the principles of a thing in composite substances" (*In Boeth. de Trinitate*, V, 3; ed. B. Decker, p. 182). Indeed, the being of a composite substance is the unity of its components. "...the being of a thing composed of matter and form ... consists in a composing of the form with the matter, or of the accident with its subject" (*In I Sent.*, d. 38, q. 1, a. 3; ed. Mandonnet, I, p. 903). See J. Owens, *op. cit.*, pp. 49-50, 73-74.

there must be a reality that is the cause of being for all other things, because it is pure being.[17] If this were not so, we would go on to infinity in causes, for everything that is not pure being has a cause of its being, as has been said. It is evident, then, that an intelligence is form and being, and that it holds its being from the first being, which is being in all its purity; and this is the first cause, or God.

[8] Everything that receives something from another is potential with regard to what it receives, and what is received in it is its actuality. The quiddity or form, therefore, which is the intelligence, must be potential with regard to the being it receives from God, and this being is received as an actuality. Thus potency and act are found in the intelligences, but not form and matter, except in an equivocal sense.[18] So, too, 'to suffer', 'to receive', 'to be a subject', and all similar expressions which seem to be attributed to things because of matter, are understood in an equivocal sense of intellectual and corporeal substances, as the Commentator remarks.[19]

[9] Because, as we have said,[20] the quiddity of an intelligence is the intelligence itself, its quiddity or essence is

[17] God is pure being (esse tantum), being itself (ipsum esse), subsistent being (esse subsistens). He is not a being (ens), that is to say, a thing that participates in being in a finite way. See In Librum de Causis, 6; ed. H. D. Saffrey, p. 47; Summa Theologiae, I, 44, 1; I, 13, 11; De Substantiis Separatis, 8; ed. F. Lescoe, § 42, p. 79. See E. Gilson, The Christian Philosophy of St. Thomas Aquinas (New York, 1955), pp. 84-95; Elements of Christian Philosophy (New York, 1960), pp. 124-133.

[18] See De Substantiis Separatis, ibid., § 44, pp. 81-82; Summa Theologiae, I, 50, 2, ad 3; De Spiritualibus Creaturis, 1. See E. Gilson, The Christian Philosophy of St. Thomas Aquinas, pp. 162-168.

[19] Averroes, In III De Anima, t. c. 14, fol. 168vb9.

[20] See above, ch. 4, § 4, p. 54.

identical with that which it is, while its being, which is received from God, is that by which it subsists in reality.[21] That is why some say that a substance of this kind is composed of 'that by which it is' (*quo est*) and 'that which is' (*quod est*),[22] or, according to Boethius, of 'that which is' (*quod est*) and 'being' (*esse*).[23]

[10]   Since there is both potency and act in the intelligences, it will not be difficult to find a multitude of them, which would be impossible if they had no potentiality. That is why the Commentator says[24] that if the nature of the possible intellect were unknown, we could not find a multitude of separate substances. These substances, moreover, are distinct from one another according to their degree of potency and act, a superior intelligence, being closer to the primary being, having more act and less po-

---

[21] To subsist means to exist *per se*, that is, through itself and not in a substance as in a subject. In short, it is the mode of being of a substance. See *In I Sent.*, d. 23, q. 1, a. 1; ed. Mandonnet, p. 555.

[22] See William of Auxerre, *In I Sent.*, c. 5, q. 4 (Paris, 1500), fol. 11a; Alexander of Hales (?), *Summa Theologica*, I-II, Inq. II, Tr. II, q. unica, n. 106 (Quaracchi, II, p. 135); St. Bonaventure, *In II Sent.*, d. 3, p. 1, a. 1, q. 1 (Quaracchi, II, p. 91); St. Albert, *In II Sent.*, d. 1A, a. 4; ed. Borgnet, 27, p. 14. See also Walter H. Principe, *William of Auxerre's Theology of the Hypostatic Union* (Toronto, 1963), pp. 22-25, 39-40, 42; *Alexander of Hales' Theology of the Hypostatic Union* (Toronto, 1967), pp. 30-40, 46-49. For these scholastics *quod est* is the concrete subject (e.g., man); *quo est* is the essence or nature by which it is what it is (e.g. humanity). See M. D. Roland-Gosselin, *op. cit.*, p. 167.

[23] *De Hebdomadibus*; PL 64, 1311C. Gilbert of Poitiers, commenting on this work of Boethius, uses the term *quo est* for the Boethian *esse*. For both, *esse* is the form or nature by which a concrete substance, such as man, is what it is; for example, humanity. See *The Commentaries on Boethius by Gilbert of Poitiers*, ed. Nicholas Häring (Toronto, 1966), pp. 194-202. For the Boethian doctrine of being, see H. Brosch, *Der Seinsbegriff bei Boethius* (Innsbruck, 1931); M. D. Roland-Gosselin, *op. cit.*, pp. 142-145. St. Thomas was aware of this meaning of *quo est*; see *In I Sent.*, d. 8, q. 5, a. 2; ed. Mandonnet, I, p. 229.

[24] Averroes, *In III De Anima*, t. c. 5, fol. 166ra16.

tency, and so with the others. This gradation ends with the human soul, which holds the lowest place among intellectual substances. As a result, its possible intellect bears the same relation to intelligible forms that primary matter, which holds the lowest position in sensible being, bears to sensible forms, as the Commentator says.[25] That is why the Philosopher compares the possible intellect to a blank tablet on which nothing is written.[26] Having more potentiality than other intellectual substances, the human soul is so close to matter that a material reality is induced to share its own being, so that from soul and body there results one being in the one composite, though this being, as belonging to the soul, does not depend on the body.[27] After this form, which is the soul, there are found other forms which have more potentiality and are even closer to matter, to such a point that they do not have being without matter. Among these forms, too, we find an order and a gradation, ending in the primary forms of the elements, which are closest to matter. For this reason they operate only as required by the active and passive qualities and other factors that dispose matter to receive form.

---

[25] *Ibid.*, fol. 160vb42.

[26] Aristotle, *De Anima*, III, 4, 430a1.

[27] Man is a unity because he has one being, which is the spiritual being that belongs in full right to the soul and which the soul communicates to the body. See St. Thomas, *Quaest. Disp. De Anima*, 1, ad 1; *Contra Gentiles*, II, 68, § 3-5. See also E. Gilson, *The Christian Philosophy of St. Thomas Aquinas*, pp. 196-197, 470, note 31. It has been well said that man's "total reality is sustained within a spiritual principle exercising a spiritual existence." A. C. Pegis, *At the Origins of the Thomistic Notion of Man* (New York, 1963), p. 37.

Chapter Five

ESSENCE AS FOUND IN DIFFERENT BEINGS

[1] From what has been said we can see how essence is found in different things. There are in fact three ways in which substances have essence. There is a reality, God, whose essence is his very being.[1] This explains why we find some philosophers who claim that God does not have a quiddity or essence, because his essence is not other than his being.[2] From this it follows that he is not in a genus, for everything in a genus must have a quiddity in addition to its being. The reason for this is that the quiddity or nature of a genus or species does not differ, as regards the notion of the nature, in the individuals in the genus or species, whereas being is diverse in these different individuals.[3]

[2] If we say that God is pure being, we need not fall into the mistake of those who held that God is that universal being by which everything formally exists.[4] The being that

[1] See above, ch. 4, § 6, 7, pp. 55-57.
[2] See Avicenna, *Metaph.*, VIII, 4, fol. 99rb; fol. 99vb; IX, 1, fol. 101va. See also William of Auvergne, *De Trinitate*, 4; *Opera Omnia*, II, supplementum (Orleans and Paris, 1674), fol. 6a. St. Thomas does not say that God has no essence, but that his being is his essence. See *In I Sent.*, d. 8, q. 1, a. 1; ed. Mandonnet, I, p. 195; *ibid.*, q. 4, a. 2, p. 222; *Contra Gentiles*, I, 21-22. For the significance of this doctrine, see J. Maritain, "Sur la doctrine de l'aséité divine," *Mediaeval Studies*, 4 (1943), pp. 43-44; E. Gilson, *Being and Some Philosophers*, 2nd ed. (Toronto, 1952), pp. 80-81.
[3] See *In I Sent.*, d. 8, q. 4, a. 2; ed. Mandonnet, I, p. 222; *ibid.*, d. 19, q. 4, a. 2, p. 483; *Contra Gentiles*, I, 25, § 4-5; *De Veritate*, 27, 1, ad 8; *Compendium Theologiae*, 14. For other texts, see L. Sweeney, "Existence/Essence in Thomas Aquinas's Early Writings," *Proceedings of the American Catholic Philosophical Ass'n*, 37, 1963, pp. 109-112. See also J. Owens, "Diversity and Community of Being in St. Thomas Aquinas," *Mediaeval Studies*, 22 (1960), pp. 257-302.
[4] Amaury of Bène, professor of logic and theology at the University of Paris,

is God is such that no addition can be made to it. Because of its purity, therefore, it is being distinct from all other being. That is why the commentary on the *Book of Causes* says that the first cause, which is pure being, is individuated through its pure goodness.[5] But even though the notion of universal being does not include any addition, it implies no prescinding from an addition. If it did, we could not conceive anything existing in which there would be an addition to being.[6]

[3] Furthermore, although God is pure being, it is not necessary that he lack other perfections or excellences. On the contrary, he possesses all the perfections of every kind of thing, so that he is called absolutely perfect, as the

---

who died about 1206 or 1207, was accused of holding this position. St. Thomas refers to it in *Summa Theologiae*, I, 3, 8, and *Contra Gentiles*, I, 26. In 1210 it was officially condemned as pantheistic. See G. C. Capelle, *Autour du décret de 1210: III. - Amaury de Bène* (Paris, 1932), pp. 42-50. On Amaury of Bène, see E. Gilson, *History of Christian Philosophy in the Middle Ages* (New York, 1955), pp. 240-241, 654, note 8.

Although William of Auvergne avoids pantheism by clearly distinguishing between God and creatures, nevertheless he taught that all things exist by the divine existence. See *De Trinitate*, 6, fol. 7b. According to him, God is in the world as the soul is in the body (*op. cit.*, 7, fol. 8b-9a). For St. Thomas, this implies that the being of God is the formal principle of all things. See *Summa Theologiae*, I-II, 17, 8, ad 2; 110, 1, ad 2.

[5] *Liber de Causis*, ed. O. Bardenhewer, 8, p. 173. See St. Thomas, *In Librum de Causis*, prop. 9; ed. H. D. Saffrey, pp. 64-66.

[6] St. Thomas distinguishes between the divine being, which by nature is pure being (*esse tantum*), and common being (*esse commune*), which is a notion abstracting from all differences of being. Since the divine being is unlimited and all-perfect, no addition can be made to it; the notion of common being allows the addition of generic and specific concepts. See *In I Sent.*, d. 8, q. 4, a. 1, ad 1; ed. Mandonnet, I, p. 219; *De Potentia*, VII, 2, ad 6; *Contra Gentiles*, I, 26 § 11; *Summa Theologiae*, I, 3, 4, ad 1. See also J. Owens, *An Elementary Christian Metaphysics* (Milwaukee, 1963), p. 81, note 3; "Diversity and Community of Being in St. Thomas Aquinas," *Mediaeval Studies*, 22 (1960), pp. 257-302.

Philosopher and Commentator say.[7] In fact, he possesses
these perfections in a more excellent way than other things,
because in him they are one, whereas in other things they
are diversified. This is because all these perfections belong
to him in virtue of his simple being.[8] In the same way if
someone could produce the operations of all the qualities
through one quality alone, in that one quality he would
possess every quality.[9] Similarly, God possesses all perfections is his being itself.

[4]   Essence is found in a second way in created intellectual
substances. Their being is other than their essence, though
their essence is without matter. Hence their being is not
separate but received, and therefore it is limited and restricted
to the capacity of the recipient nature. But their nature or
quiddity is separate and not received in matter. That is why
the *Book of Causes* says that the intelligences are unlimited
from below and limited from above.[10] They are, in fact,
limited as to their being, which they receive from a higher
reality, but they are not limited from below, because their
forms are not limited to the capacity of a matter that receives them.

[5]   That is why among these substances we do not find a

---

[7] Aristotle, *Metaph.*, V, 16, 1021b30; Averroes, *In V Metaph.*, t. c. 21,
fol. 62ra10-13.

[8] See *Summa Theologiae*, I, 4, 2; *Contra Gentiles*, I, 28.

[9] By quality is meant power, the immediate source of a thing's operation.
Fire, for example, warms through its quality of heat. If fire could also cool,
and do everything else, through this one quality, this power would include
all power. On this analogy God has unlimited power of being (*virtus essendi*)
through his *esse*. See *Contra Gentiles*, I, 28, §, 1, 2.

[10] *Liber de Causis*, 4; *ed. cit.*, p. 167. See St. Thomas, *In Librum de Causis*,
prop. 4, ed. H. D. Saffrey, p. 30; prop. 5, p. 39. *De Substantiis Separatis*, 8,
ed. L. Lescoe, § 45, p. 82. *Summa Theologiae*, I, 50, 2, ad 4.

multitude of individuals in the same species, as has been said,[11] except in the case of the human soul because of the body to which it is united. And even though the individuation of the soul depends on the body as for the occasion of its beginning, because it acquires its individuated being only in the body of which it is the actuality, it is not necessary that the individuation cease when the body is removed. Because the soul has a separate being, once the soul has acquired its individuated being by having been made the form of a particular body, that being always remains individuated. That is why Avicenna says that the individuation and multiplication of souls depends on the body as regards its beginning but not as regards its end.[12]

[6] Furthermore, because the quiddity of these substances is not identical with their being, they can be classified in a category. For this reason they have a genus, species, and difference, though their specific differences are hidden from us.[13] Even in the case of sensible things we do not know their essential differences;[14] we indicate them through the accidental differences that flow from the essential differences, as we refer to a cause through its effect. In this way 'biped' is given as the difference of man. We are ignorant, however, of the proper accidents of immaterial substances; so we can designate their differences neither through themselves nor through accidental differences.

[7] We must observe that the genus and difference are

[11] See above, ch. 4, § 5, p. 54.
[12] Avicenna, De Anima, V, 3, fol. 14rb.
[13] See St. Thomas, In II Sent., d. 3, q. 1, a. 4; ed. Mandonnet, II, pp. 99-100.
[14] See ibid., a. 6, p. 104; De Veritate, 4, 1, ad 8; 10, 1, ad 6; Contra Gentiles, I, 3, § 5; In VII Metaph., lect. 12, § 1552.

not derived in the same way in these substances and in sensible substances.[15] In sensible substances the genus is obtained from the material side of the thing, whereas the difference is obtained from its formal side. That is why Avicenna says[16] that in substances composed of matter and form, the form is the simple difference of that which is constituted by it; not that the form itself is the difference but that it is the principle of the difference, as he says in his *Metaphysics*.[17] A difference of this kind is called a simple difference because it is derived from a part of the quiddity of the thing, namely its form. But since immaterial substances are simple quiddities, we cannot take their difference from a part of the quiddity, but from the whole quiddity. As Avicenna says, only those species have a simple difference whose essences are composed of matter and form.[18]

[8] The genus of immaterial substances is also obtained from the whole essence, though in a different way. Separate substances are like one another in being immaterial, but they differ in their degree of perfection, depending on their distance from potentiality and their closeness to pure act. Their genus, then, is derived from what follows upon their immateriality, as for example intellectuality, or something of this sort. Their difference, which in fact is unknown to us, is derived from what follows upon their degree of perfection.

[9] These differences need not be accidental because they are determined by degrees of perfection, which do not diversity the species. True, the degree of perfection in

[15] See *In II Sent.*, d. 3, q. 1, a. 5-6; ed. Mandonnet, II, pp. 98-106.
[16] Avicenna, *op. cit.*, I, 1, fol. 1rb.
[17] Avicenna, *Metaph.*, V, 6, fol. 90rb.
[18] Avicenna, *De Anima*, I, 1, fol. 1rb.

receiving the same form does not produce different species, as for example the more white and the less white in participating whiteness of the same nature. But different degrees of perfection in the forms themselves or in the participated natures do produce different species. Nature, for example, advances by degrees from the plant to the animal world using as intermediaries types of things that are between animals and plants, as the Philosopher says.[19] Of course intellectual substances do not always have to be divided by two real differences; as the Philosopher shows, this cannot happen in all cases.[20]

[10]   In a third way essence is found in substances composed of matter and form. In these, too, being is received and limited, because they have being from another. Their nature or quiddity, moreover, is received in designated matter. Thus they are limited both from above and from below. A multitude of individuals in the same species is also possible in their case because of the division of designated matter. As for the relation of the essence of these substances to logical notions, that has been explained above.[21]

[19] *Historia Animalium,* VIII, 1, 588b4-14. Michael Scot translated Aristotle's three treatises on animals from the Arabic under the title *De Animalibus.* Books 1-10 correspond to *Historia Animalium;* 11-14 to *De Partibus Animalium.* See M. D. Roland-Gosselin, *op. cit.,* p. 42, note 1.

[20] *De Partibus Animalium,* I, 2, 642b5.

[21] See above, ch. 3.

Chapter Six

ESSENCE AS FOUND IN ACCIDENTS

[1] Now that we have explained how essence is present in all substances, it remains for us to see how essence exists in accidents. Because essence is what the definition signifies, as has been said,[1] accidents must have an essence in the same way that they have a definition. Now their definition is incomplete, because they cannot be defined without including a subject in their definition.[2] This is because they do not have being in themselves, independent of a subject; as substantial being results from form and matter when they come together, so accidental being results from an accident and a subject when the former comes to the latter. For the same reason neither a substantial form nor matter has a complete essence, because the definition of a substantial form must include the subject of the form. It is defined, therefore, by adding something outside its genus, just like the definition of an accidental form. That is also why the body is included in the definition of the soul when it is defined by the natural philosopher, who considers the soul only as the form of a physical body.

---

[1] See above, ch. 1, § 4, pp. 31-32.

[2] An accident is an essence whose nature it is to exist in a substance as in a subject. See *Summa Theologiae*, III, 77, 1, ad 2; *In VII Metaph.*, lect. 1, § 1248, lect. 4, § 1335-8; *In II De Anima*, lect. 1, § 213; *Quodl.*, IX, 5, ad 2. On the nature of accidents, see E. Gilson, *The Christian Philosophy of St. Thomas Aquinas* (New York, 1956), pp. 30-31, 177, 445, note 5; J. Owens, *An Elementary Christian Metaphysics* (Milwaukee, 1963), pp. 143-146, 155-157, 165-178; J. A. Albertson, "*Esse* of Accidents according to St. Thomas," *Modern Schoolman*, 30 (1953), pp. 265-278.

[2]   There is a considerable difference, however, between substantial and accidental forms. As a substantial form does not have being in itself, independent of that to which it is united, so neither does the matter to which it is joined. From their union results that being in which the reality subsists in itself, and from them is produced something essentially one. An essence, therefore, results from their union. It follows that although a form, considered in itself, does not have the complete nature of an essence, nevertheless it is part of a complete essence. But that to which an accident is added is a complete being in itself, subsisting in its own being; and this being is by nature prior to the supervening accident. That is why the supervening accident, by its union with the subject to which it comes, does not cause that being in which the reality subsists, and through which the reality is a being in itself. Rather, it causes a secondary being, without which we can conceive the subsistent reality to exist, as what is primary can be understood without what is secondary. So the accident and its subject do not produce something essentially, but accidentally, one. This explains why their union does not result in an essence, like the conjunction of form and matter. It also explains why an accident neither has the nature of a complete essence nor is part of a complete essence. As it is a being in a qualified sense, so it has an essence in a qualified sense.[3]

[3]   Furthermore, that which is said to be most fully and truly in a genus is the cause of everything posterior in the

---

[3] An accident is not a being (*ens*) but a being of a being (*ens entis*). Color, for instance, is the color of something. An accident does not exist, but it exists in something. Whiteness, for instance, does not exist, but things exist in a white manner. See *Summa Theologiae*, I, 28, 2; *In VII Metaph.*, lect. 1, § 1253; *In XII Metaph.*, lect. 1, § 2419; *Quodl.*, IX, 5, ad 1.

genus. For example, fire, which is the ultimate in heat, is
the cause of heat in hot things, as the *Metaphysics* says.[4]
That is why substance, which holds the first place in the
genus of being, having essence most truly and fully, must be
the cause of accidents, which share the nature of being
secondarily and in a qualified sense.

[4] This happens in different ways. The parts of substance
being matter and form, some accidents result principally
from form and others from matter.[5] There is a form whose
being does not depend on matter (for example, the intellectual soul),[6] whereas matter has being only through form.
That is why among accidents that result from form there are
some that have nothing in common with matter, as for
example understanding, which does not take place through
a bodily organ, as the Philosopher proves.[7] On the contrary,
other accidents deriving from form do have something in
common with matter, as for example sensation and the
like. But no accident results from matter without having
something in common with form.

[5] Among accidents that derive from matter we find the
following difference. Some accidents result from matter
because of its relation to a special form. Examples are male
and female among animals — a difference that is reducible
to matter, as the *Metaphysics* says.[8] That is why, once the
form of animal has been removed, these accidents no longer

---

[4] *Metaph.*, II, 1, 993b24.
[5] This is based on Avicenna, *Sufficientia*, I, 6, fol. 17b.
[6] See St. Thomas, *Quaest. Disp. De Anima*, 1.
[7] *De Anima*, III, 4, 429b3. See St. Thomas, *In III De Anima*, lect. 7.
[8] *Metaph.*, X, 9, 1058b21. See St. Thomas, *In X Metaph.*, lect. 9, § 2128-
2134.

remain except in an equivocal sense. Other accidents result from matter in its relation to a general form. In this case, when the special form is taken away, these accidents still remain in the matter. An example is the blackness of an Ethiopian's skin, which comes from the mixture of the elements and not from the nature of the soul, with the result that it remains in him after death.

[6] Because everything is individuated by matter and located in a genus or species through its form, accidents that derive from matter are accidents of the individual and they differentiate individuals within the same species. On the contrary, accidents that result from the form are properties belonging to the genus or species, and consequently they are found in everything sharing the nature of the genus or species. For example, the ability to laugh results from man's form, for laughter occurs because of some perception on the part of the human soul.

[7] Another point to notice is that accidents are sometimes caused in perfect actuality by the essential principles, like heat in fire, which is always actually hot. But sometimes accidents are caused only as aptitudes, and they are completed by an external agent, like transparency in the air, which is complemented by an external luminous body.[9] In cases like these the aptitude is an inseparable accident, whereas the completion that comes from a source external to the essence of the thing, or that does not enter into its

---

9 Transparency (*diaphaneitas*), according to Aristotle, is a nature to some extent pervading all bodies, but especially air and water, making them capable of receiving light. See Aristotle, *De Sensu*, 3, 439a17-b18; *De Anima*, II, 7, 418b4-14; St. Thomas, *In De Sensu*, lect. 5, *Opera Omnia* (New York, 1949), 20, p. 157; *In II De Anima*, lect. 14.

constitution, will be separable from it, like movement and other accidents of this kind.

[8] Still another fact worthy of notice is that genus, species, and difference are derived differently in accidents and in substances. In substances, from substantial form and matter there is constituted something essentially one, the consequence of their union being one nature that is properly in the category of substance. That is why, in the case of substances, concrete names that signify the composite are properly said to be in a category, either as a species or as a genus, as for example 'man' or 'animal'. Form or matter, on the contrary, is not in a category in this way but only by reduction, as principles are said to be in a category.[10] From an accident and its subject, however, there is not produced something essentially one. Hence the result of their union is not one nature to which the notion of genus or species can be attributed. That is why terms designating accidents concretely, like 'something white' or 'something musical', cannot be placed in a category except by reduction. They are in a category only when expressed abstractly, like 'whiteness' or 'music'.

[9] Because accidents are not composed of matter and form, we cannot take their genus from matter and their difference from form, as we do in composite substances. Rather, we must take their primary genus from their mode of being, because the term 'a being' is predicated in diverse

---

[10] Form and matter are not in a category directly or through themselves, but through the substance of which they are the principles. So too, a privation like blindness can be placed in a category only through the positive power of sight of which it is the privation. See *Summa Theologiae*, I, 3, 5; *De Veritate*, 27, 1, ad 8.

ways, by priority and posteriority, of the ten genera of the categories.[11] For example, quantity is called a being because it is the measure of substance, quality because it is the disposition of substance, and so on with the other accidents, as the Philosopher says.[12] Their differences, however, are derived from the diversity of the principles that cause them. And because properties result from the specific principles of the subject, this subject takes the place of the difference in their definition when they are defined in the abstract, which is the way they are properly in a category. For instance, we say that snubness is a curvature of the nose. But the converse would be true if we defined them in the concrete. In this case the subject would be placed in their definition as the genus, because these accidents would then be defined like composite substances, in which the concept of the genus is derived from matter. An example is calling a snub nose a curved nose. The same is true when one accident is the principle of another, as action, passion, and quantity are principles of relation. (That is why the Philosopher divides relation with reference to these in the *Metaphysics*).[13] But because the specific principles of accidents are not always evident, we sometimes take the differences of accidents from their effects, as when we say that colors are differentiated as 'dilating' and 'expanding'-

[11] See St. Thomas, *In IV Metaph.*, lect. 1, § 535-543. On the analogous predication of being see G. B. Phelan, *Saint Thomas and Analogy* (Milwaukee, 1941), (reprinted in *Selected Papers*, pp. 95-121); E. Mascall, *Existence and Analogy* (London and New York, 1949); J. F. Anderson, *The Bond of Being* (St. Louis, 1949); G. P. Klubertanz, *St. Thomas Aquinas on Analogy* (Chicago, 1960); R. M. McInerny, *The Logic of Analogy* (The Hague, 1961); J. Owens, *An Elementary Christian Metaphysics* (Milwaukee, 1963), pp. 86-93, 162.

[12] *Metaph.*, IV, 2, 1003a33-b10.

[13] *Metaph.*, V, 15, 1020b26. See St. Thomas, *In V Metaph.*, lect. 17.

differences that are caused by the abundance and scarcity of light, which produce the different species of color.[14]

[10] It is clear, then, how essence exists in substances and in accidents, and in composite and simple substances. It is also evident how the universal concepts of logic are related to all these, with the exception of the first cause, which is absolutely simple. Because of its simplicity, neither the notion of genus nor of species, nor consequently the notion of definition, applies to it. In this being may our treatise find its end and fulfillment.

---

[14] According to mediaeval physics, the different species of color are caused by different mixtures of white, which contains the most light, and black, which contains the least. Because the essential differences of colors are unknown, colors are distinguished by their effects. A color having an abundance of white, and consequently of light, dilates or increases vision; a color having an abundance of black, and thus lacking light, contracts or decreases vision. See Plato, *Timaeus*, 67E; Aristotle, *Metaph.*, X, 7, 1057b8-18; St. Thomas, *In X Metaph.*, lect. 3, § 1968; lect. 9, § 2106, 2107.

BIBLIOGRAPHY

Editions and Translations of De Ente et Essentia

Allers, Rudolf, *Thomas von Aquin, Über das Sein und das Wesen*, übersetzt und erläutert von Rudolf Allers (Koln & Olten, 1956).

Baur, Ludwig, *Sermo seu Tractatus De Ente et Essentia*, edidit Ludovicus Baur, editio altera emendata, *Opuscula et Textus, Series Scholastica*, I (Münster i. West., 1933).

Bobik, Joseph, *Aquinas On Being and Essence, a Translation and Interpretation* (Notre Dame, Indiana, 1965).

Boyer, Charles, *Opusculum De Ente et Essentia*, introductione et notis auctum edidit C. Boyer, *Textus et Documenta, Series Philosophica*, 5 (Rome, 1933).

Bruneteau, Emile, *De Ente et Essentia*, texte latin, précédé d'une introduction, accompagné d'une traduction, et d'un double commentaire historique et philosophique par Emile Bruneteau (Paris, 1914).

Capelle, Catherine, *L'Etre et l'Essence*, traduction et notes par Sr. Catherine Capelle, O.P., *Bibliothèque des textes philosophiques* (Paris, 1947).

Kendzierski, L. H. and Wade, F. C., *Cajetan, Commentary On Being and Essence (In De Ente et Essentia D. Thomae Aquinatis)*, translated from the Latin with an Introduction (Milwaukee, 1964).

Leckie, George, *Concerning Being and Essence* (New York, 1937).

Lituma, Luis, and Wagner de Reyna, Alberto, *Del Ente y De la Esencia, Biblioteca Filosófica*, traducción del latin (Buenos Aires, 1940).

Mandonnet, Pierre, *De Ente et Essentia, Opuscula Omnia S. Thomae Aquinatis*, I, cura et studio R. P. Petri Mandonnet, O.P. (Paris, 1927).

Miano, Vincenzo, *Dell' Ente et dell' Essenza*, introduzione, traduzione et note di Vincenzo Miano (Turin, 1952).

Perrier, Joannes, *De Ente et Essentia, Opuscula Omnia*, I (Paris, 1949).

Riedl, Clare, *On Being and Essence, St. Michael's College Philosophical Texts*. Revised edition (Toronto, 1937).

Roland-Gosselin, M. D., *Le "De Ente et Essentia" de S. Thomas d'Aquin. Texte établi d'après les manuscrits Parisiens*. Introduction, notes et études historiques par M. D. Roland-Gosselin, O.P., *Bibliothèque Thomiste*, VIII (Le Saulchoir, Kain, Belgium, 1926).

Sepich, Juan, *El Ente y La Esencia*, Texto Latino y Traducción Castellana, prólogo de Tomás D. Casares, estudio preliminar, traducción y notas por Juan R. Sepich. *Clásicos de la Filosofía*, II (Buenos Aires, 1940).

Other Works of St. Thomas Aquinas

For the editions and translations of the works of St. Thomas, see I. T. Eschmann, "A Catalogue of St. Thomas's Works," in Etienne Gilson, *The Christian Philosophy of St. Thomas Aquinas* (New York, 1956), pp. 381-430.

St. Thomas Aquinas, *Opera Omnia*, ed. Leonine, 16 vols. (Rome, 1882-1948). *Expositio in libros Peri Hermenias, Commentaria in libros Posteriorum Analyticorum*, vol. 1; *in libros De Caelo et Mundo*, vol. 3; *Summa Theologiae*, vols. 4-12; *Contra Gentiles*, vols. 13-15.

Summa Theologiae, Latin text and English translation, introductions, notes, appendices, and glossaries (Cambridge, England and New York, 1964-).

On the Truth of the Catholic Faith (Summa Contra Gentiles), trans. by A. C. Pegis, J. F. Anderson, V. J. Bourke, C. O'Neil, 5 vols. (New York, 1955-1957).

Basic Writings of Saint Thomas, ed. A. C. Pegis, 2 vols. (New York, 1945).

An Introduction to the Metaphysics of St. Thomas Aquinas, Texts selected and translated by J. F. Anderson (Chicago, 1953).

The Pocket Aquinas, Selections from the Writings of St. Thomas, ed. V. J. Bourke (New York, 1960).

The Wisdom and Ideas of Saint Thomas Aquinas, ed. E. Freeman and J. Owens (New York, 1968).

Aristotle: On Interpretation: Commentary by St. Thomas and Cajetan (Perihermenias), trans. with an introduction by J. T. Oesterle (Milwaukee, 1962).

Expositio in libros Metaphysicorum, ed. M. R. Cathala and R. M. Spiazzi (Turin, 1950).

Commentary on the Metaphysics of Aristotle, trans. by J. P. Rowan, 3 vols. (Chicago, 1961).

Scriptum super libros Sententiarum Magistri Petri Lombardi, ed. P. Mandonnet and M. F. Moos, 4 vols. (Paris, 1929-1947).

Quaestiones Disputatae, 9th edition, ed. R. Spiazzi et al. (Turin and Rome, 1953). *De Veritate*, vol. 1; *De Potentia Dei*, *De Spiritualibus Creaturis*, vol. 2.

De Spiritualibus Creaturis, ed. Leo W. Keeler (Rome, 1937).

On Spiritual Creatures, trans. by M. C. Fitzpatrick (Milwaukee, 1949).

On the Power of God, trans. by the Dominican Fathers (Westminster, Maryland, 1952).

Truth, trans. by R. W. Mulligan, J. V. McGlynn, and R. W. Schmidt, 3 vols. (Chicago, 1954).

Quaestiones De Anima, ed. J. Robb (Toronto, 1968).

De Substantiis Separatis, edited and trans. by F. J. Lescoe (West Hartford, Connecticut, 1963).

Commentarium in librum De Anima, ed. A. M. Pirotta (Turin, 1936).

Aristotle's De Anima in the Version of William of Moerbeke and the Commentary of St. Thomas Aquinas, trans. by K. Foster and S. Humphries (London, 1951).

De Unitate Intellectus contra Averroistas, ed. Leo Keeler (Rome, 1936).

Quaestiones Quodlibetales, ed. P. Mandonnet (Paris, 1926).

Opuscula Omnia, ed. P. Mandonnet, 5 vols. (Paris, 1927).

Opuscula Philosophica, ed. R. M. Spiazzi (Turin, Rome, 1954).

Opuscula Omnia necnon Opera Minora, vol. 1, ed. J. Perrier (Paris, 1949).

Expositio super librum Boethii De Trinitate, ed. B. Decker (Leiden, 1955).

The Division and Methods of the Sciences: Questions V and VI of St. Thomas' Commentary on the De Trinitate of Boethius, trans. with introduction and notes by A. Maurer, 3rd ed. (Toronto, 1963).

Super librum De Causis Expositio, ed. H. D. Saffrey (Fribourg, Louvain, 1954).

Select Readings

Bourke, Vernon, J., *Aquinas' Search for Wisdom* (Milwaukee, 1965).

Chenu, M. D., *Toward Understanding St. Thomas*, trans. by A. M. Landry and D. Hughes (Chicago, 1964).

Fabro, Cornelio, *La Nozione Metafisica di Partecipazione secondo S. Tommaso d'Aquino*, 3rd ed. (Turin, 1963).

——, *Participation et Causalité selon S. Thomas d'Aquin* (Louvain, Paris, 1961).

Finance, Joseph de, *Etre et Agir dans la Philosophie de Saint Thomas* (Paris, 1945).

Geiger, Louis, B., *La Participation dans la Philosophie de S. Thomas d'Aquin* (Paris, 1942).

Gilson, Etienne, *Being and Some Philosophers*, 2nd ed. (Toronto, 1952).

——, *History of Christian Philosophy in the Middle Ages* (New York, 1955).

——, *The Christian Philosophy of St. Thomas Aquinas*, trans. by L. K. Shook (New York, 1956). Contains a catalogue of St. Thomas' works by I. T. Eschmann.

——, *Elements of Christian Philosophy* (New York, 1960).

——, *Le Thomisme*, 6th ed. (Paris, 1965).

Grabmann, Martin, "Die Schrift 'De Ente et Essentia' und die Seinsmetaphysik des h. Thomas von Aquin," *Mittelalterliches Geistesleben*, I (Munich, 1926).

——, "De Commentariis in Opusculum S. Thomae Aquinatis De Ente et Essentia," *Acta Pontificiae Academiae Romanae* (Vatican, 1938).

Lynch, Lawrence, *A Christian Philosophy* (New York, 1968).

Maritain, Jacques, *Existence and the Existent*, trans. by L. Galantière and G. B. Phelan (New York, 1948).

——, *A Preface to Metaphysics* (London, 1943).

Maurer, Armand, *Medieval Philosophy* (New York, 1962).

Owens, Joseph, *An Elementary Christian Metaphysics* (Milwaukee, 1963).

——, *An Interpretation of Existence* (Milwaukee, 1968).

Pegis, Anton, C., *St. Thomas and the Greeks* (Milwaukee, 1939).

Phelan, Gerald, B., *Selected Papers*, ed. A. G. Kirn (Toronto, 1967).

Pieper, Josef, *Guide to Thomas Aquinas*, trans. by R. and C. Winston (New York, 1962).

Schmidt, Robert, *The Domain of Logic according to Saint Thomas Aquinas* (The Hague, 1966).

Smith, Gerard, *Natural Theology: Metaphysics* II (New York, 1951).

——, and Kendzierski, Lottie, *The Philosophy of Being: Metaphysics* I (New York, 1961).

Walz, Angelus, *Saint Thomas Aquinas, a Biographical Study*, trans. by S. Bullough (Westminster, Maryland, 1951).

INDEX

Abstraction, 32, 39.

Accident, definition 66, has incomplete essence 66-67, a being in qualified sense 32-33, 67, causes secondary being 67, of individual and species 69, separable and inseparable 69-70, relation to logical notions 70.

Accidental form, differs from substantial 67.

Albert, St., 52, 58.

Albertson, J. A., 66.

Alexander of Hales, 51, 58.

Alfarabi, 10.

Amaury of Bène, 60-61.

Analogy of being, 70-71.

Anderson, J. F., 71.

Angels, 51 (see intelligences).

Aristotle (Philosopher), 28, 29, 31, 41, 45, 52, 59, 62, 65, 68, 69, 71.

Averroes (Commentator), 30, 34, 35, 37, 42, 48, 57-59, 62.

Avicebron, 20, 51.

Avicenna, 8, 9, 11, 28, 31, 35, 37, 40, 43, 45, 46, 48, 52, 54, 60, 63, 64.

Barrett, W., 14, 30.

Baur, L., 27.

Being, a (*ens*), 9, 14-17, 29-30, 32.

Being (*esse*), actuality of essence 9, perfection and primacy of 10, 11, 32, meaning 14, 15, difference between divine being and common being 61.

Blanche, F. A., 39.

Bobik, J., 21.

Body, two meanings, 38, 39.

Boethius, 15, 31, 35, 37, 58.

Bonaventure, St., 51, 58.

Book of Causes (*Liber de Causis*), 53, 61, 62.

Bourke, V., 8, 75.

Brosch, H., 58.

Capelle, G. C., 61.

Certitudo, 31.

Chenu, M. D., 8, 11, 75.

Collins, J., 51.

Color, Aristotelian theory of 71-72.

Commentator (see Averroes).

Difference, second intention 12, 28, derived from form 40-41, relation to essence 45-50.

Ens (see a being), derivation and meaning 13-16, *ens per se* and *ens per accidens* 30.

Eschmann, I. T., 74.

Esse (see being), derivation and meaning 14-19.

Essence, meaning 15-16, 30-32, potential to being 32, signified by definition 34, according to which a thing is said to be 36, twofold consideration of 46, in God 61-62, in intellectual substances 62, in material substances 65, in accidents 66-67, distinct from being in created substances 20-23, 26, 55, relation to logical notions 45-50.

Essentia (see essence), derivation 32.

Fabro, C., 21, 53, 55, 75.

Finance, J. de, 76.

Form, determination of a thing 31, actuality of matter 34-35, of whole and of part 31, role in individuation 37.

Geiger, L. B., 76.

Genus, second intention 12, 28, differs from species 37-38, derived from matter 41, signifies whole essence 42, relation to essence 45-50.

Gerard of Abbeyville, 51.

Gilbert of Poitiers, 58.

Gillet, St. M., 20.

Gilson, E., 10, 14, 15, 20, 24, 25, 32, 33, 37, 51, 52, 57, 59, 60, 61, 66, 76.

God, pure being 9, 18, 60, existence of 23-27, not a substance 33, not in a

Question 324

Meta - 8:00
Kis - 10:30

Dan - Thur 10:30